# THE REPUBLICAN PARTY

# AND

# THE CONSTITUTION

# THE REPUBLICAN PARTY,

# THE CONSTITUTION,

# AND

# THE DECLINE OF AMERICA

Sam Kushner

# Acknowledgements

I am grateful to Richard Buxbaum, my former law professor and a friend, for going through the script,  and for his encouragement.

# CONTENTS

# Preface

1. **About the Book.** At one place and in a few pages, this book provides comprehensive information for Independents, Democrats and Republicans voters which is not available anywhere else. Millions of Republican voters think that the Party stands for low taxes and "family values," but that's just the tip of the iceberg. Few know about the Party's ideology, the "free markets," or about "de-funding," "starving the beast," and about the secret organization that controls the Party. How many know about Dominionism and the Federalist Society, about the connection between the Neo-Conservatives (who advocated attack on Iraq long before invasion) and Machiavelli? How many know there is no separation of powers now? The insights will surprise and intrigue you.

2. **The Forty Year Window.** Detecting a pattern in what we intermittently see and hear is not in our genes. So a period of 40 years (1970-2011) is covered here—to connect the dots. Just looking at the GW Bush's record tells us little: huge tax cuts for the rich, an unwarranted 4 trillion expenditure on war; now compare it to Reagan's huge expenditures on science fiction--the SDI, reckless military expansion in peacetime and raising the national debt limit by trillions. Suddenly, the ideology, the strategy, the tactics fall into place. In the past when both the parties worked for democracy, there was no pattern to detect. The voters still vote on that assumption. We believe what the Party tells us: Washington is broken/Party politics as usual/Social Security and Medicare, and labor unions are the problems. But when the dots are connected, we know Washington is not broken. It has been broken. Why? It is a fascinating story.

3. **Repetition.** Even a casual reader will notice some repetitive matter. Reagan as a leader is examined in the chapter on Party's history, then again in the chapter on GOP Fiscal Record. Fullness of information in the context of the chapter is the reason so the reader does not have to keep looking back.

4. **Bias.** The book reads like a diatribe. Consider: America was set up as a democracy and has functioned as such from 1787 to 1970 (except during the Civil War). Now if one of the parties secretly starts to dismantle democracy and ceases to represent the people, should one defend its actions? Applaud it? Can Bernie Madoff's actions be defended? The Democrats' incompetence and lack of vigilance is mind boggling. Having said that, the question is: should a Party commit burglary because it can?

5. **K.I.S.S (Keep it Simple, Simon!).** The philosophy of the book is to minimize the distractions created by endless references, tables etc. It is a narrative of facts and events in simple language to be easily intelligible. It is for the 99%. Hence references have been minimized or included in the text. The goal here is: inform--don't impress. The purpose is to give the reader the tools to connect the dots. Then he can make his choice based on information.

# I

## AN ICEBERG SHOCKS THE TITANIC

*Advocates of capitalism are very apt to appeal to the sacred principles of liberty, which are embodied in one maxim: The fortunate must not be restrained in the exercise of tyranny over the unfortunate.*—Bertrand Russell

Ⓞ

A beacon of freedom and liberty to the world, America achieved its lofty perch due to its great leaders: Washington, Jefferson, John Adams, Lincoln, Theodore Roosevelt, and Franklin Roosevelt. They set up the conditions that unleashed the people's ingenuity and hard work, and the American democracy flourished. America tackled every challenge head on.

As early as the 1830s, Tocqueville noticed in *Democracy in America* that in contrast to the European aristocratic ethic, "America was a society where hard work and money-making was the dominant ethic, where the common man enjoyed a level of dignity which was unprecedented, where commoners never deferred to elites." He also noticed that in America, capitalism was tempered by public good.

Now it sounds like an American folklore. Today, America can't solve its problems after the economic meltdown in 2008—the result of an uncontrolled Wall Street. America has been fighting an unwinnable war in Afghanistan after spending trillions on the Iraq war. The national debt is over 14 trillion dollars. The unemployment is high, economy is stagnant, and the infrastructure is crumbling. Its manufacturing base has been decimated in the last thirty years, and replaced by a large get-rich-quick at any cost financial sector. While educational standards are falling, costs keep skyrocketing, and healthcare is a mess. Environment issues have been debated for two decades but remain unaddressed. Poverty is increasing; income disparities have increased to the level of late 1900s. Top 1% own quarter of national income and over one third of national wealth. In the 1970s the CEO's earned 40 times the average worker's wage, today they earn over 300 times. It's democracy in reverse.

When the President is Republican, trillions are doled out in tax cuts to the rich and the public is told: deficits don't matter! When a Democrat is in the White House, the battle cry changes: fix deficits first and no tax increases! The Republican Party's ideology of "free markets and small government" aims to dismantle Social Security, Medicare, labor unions and privatize healthcare, education, and other institutions. But democracy is not an ideology; the Constitution has no ideology. The recent debt-ceiling deal debate showed to the world that the US political system is broken. At a time when public spending is needed to grow the economy, the debt reduction deal between the two parties cut government spending. Bill Gross, PIMCO's legendary bond fund manager, wrote in an article on PIMCO blog in June,'11 that the parties should be investing in the country's needs to create jobs and to compete globally over the next 25-50 years. For that to happen, the government needs to take a larger role —not a smaller one —in the economy—at least for now. The spending cuts will further increase the income gap and shrink the middle class which has been the engine of America's growth.

In the report, *Age of America Nears End* (April *25*, 2011) International Monetary Fund said, China's economy will surpass the U.S. in 2016. The Chinese economy will expand from $11.2 trillion this year to $19 trillion in 2016. The U.S. economy will grow from $15.2 to $18.8 trillion. Just 10 years ago, when GW Bush came to power, the U.S. economy was three times the size of China's economy.

More than the economy is at stake. The core American values—equal economic opportunity, free basic public education, and the American dream—are fading away. Public has lost trust in Congress, politicians, banks, and in the government.

Hendrik Hertzberg, senior editor at *The New Yorker* (*The Road Ahead for Progressives, The Nation, 13 October 2010 by LaMarche*), incisively sums up the situation: "... The Obama experience, in my view, has highlighted the immensity of the structural barriers to reform—the 'separation of powers,' the filibuster and other Senate horrors, federalism, the electoral system at all levels, the power of money. This is the sort of thing that is catching up with us, big time. Not a pretty picture."

Perhaps, the problem can be framed more narrowly. Why has the national debt skyrocketed in the last thirty years? Why a party known for fiscal conservatism has become fiscally reckless? Why is the Democrat Party unable to carry out its agenda even after a convincing victory in 2008 elections? Who is to blame? The Constitution? The Democrats? The Republicans? The media?

The book briefly discusses these issues to provide a perspective to people who are puzzled: Why Washington does not work?

The Decline of America

# II

## THE WIZARDS OF PHILADELPHIA

*"I hear America singing."*—Walt Whitman

Ⓞ

Given the difficult conditions facing them, it is a marvel that the Framers were able to piece together a document that has served America so well. It worked because all the branches of government wanted it to work. If the same task had been entrusted to a group of people with the caliber of today's Congress, what would be the result? Democrats would still be growing tobacco in Virginia, and the Republicans selling Jesus, guns and soap to the world.

The Constitution was a great document. It worked magnificently for about two centuries. The question is: is it working now? Let's ask another question: is the rocket that put us on the moon, fit for mission to Mars?

### THE REASON FOR THE CONSTITUTION

The Constitution describes briefly the procedure for forming a legitimate government, and then it allocates power between the states and the federal government, and among the three branches of government: legislature, executive, and judicial. Its purpose was to ensure the protection of the natural rights of men, i.e. equality, life (security), liberty, and pursuit of happiness, and to protect the people from a tyrannical government.

## HOW THE CONSTITUTION WAS COBBLED?

While the war of independence was still going on, Benjamin Franklin suggested that the colonies meet and discuss their grievances against the British. On July 4, 1776, the representatives passed the Declaration of Independence: all men are created equal and have the rights of Life, Liberty, and Happiness, and that governments without the consent of the governed are illegitimate. After the Declaration, each colony was sovereign and formed a constitution. The Articles of Confederation were drawn up to co-ordinate foreign policy and the war effort. After victory over the British in 1782, a peace treaty was signed in Paris in 1783. And America was born. Now it needed a Constitution that would take into account the interests of various states and create a strong national government.

At the initiative of Madison and Alexander Hamilton, fifty-five delegates were invited from the 13 states to the Convention at Philadelphia in May, 1787. Framers were aware of the historic nature of their undertaking. Among the delegates were men whose greatness—and foibles—are well known today: George Washington (whose ambition lurked just below the surface); Alexander Hamilton (John Adams called him "the bastard son of a Scotch peddler"); James Madison (so reticent that his sparkling wife Dolly had to do all the talking); Benjamin Franklin (who almost electrocuted himself while attempting to electrocute a turkey because for a moment he forgot the difference). John Adams (irascible, cantankerous, and argumentative), and Thomas Jefferson (his slave Sally Hemings gave him a few children whom he freed on his death-bed. But not Sally Hemings)—the would-be presidents—were away as envoys to Britain and France, but kept in touch with the delegates. All men were determined not to let the Convention fail—even if that meant swallowing personal pride and giving up some of their long held principles.

It is important not to think of Constitution as a document crafted on lofty principles. There were heated debates on issues like separation of powers, the composition of House and the Senate, on the powers of President, on the method of presidential election, and the tenure of office holders. There were moments when the Convention was on breaking point. In the end, however, it was pieced together by old-fashioned horse-trading—and the fear of reaching no agreement at all.

## THE PIVOT: SEPARATION OF POWERS

The Framers were intellectuals and pragmatic at the same time. Having never seen a working democracy, they drew on their reading, experience of the colonies, and their observation of the English government. The doctrine of separation of powers was originally developed by Polybius (200-118 BC), a Greek, from his observation of the Roman Republic. Polybius believed that by itself, each of the three forms—monarchy (rule by the one), aristocracy (rule by the few), and democracy (rule by the many)—will end up in tyranny. His solution was to mix the three—in a kind of political cocktail—in a single government so that each checked and balanced the other two. The doctrine had influenced the political thinking of their contemporaries like Montesquieu, Locke, Blackstone, Hume, Harrington, and others.

After closely observing the English government, they convinced themselves that it was the separation of powers that kept the British government in balance: the monarch checked, and in turn, was checked by the Parliament, the House of Commons by the House of Lords and vice-versa. The House of Lords worked as an independent highest court.

So the doctrine became the centerpiece of the Constitution. The President cannot legislate without the Congress; and Congress cannot pass a bill without the President's assent (by a

11

supermajority the Congress can override the veto). It is a symbiotic relationship. While specifying the powers of Federal government, the Constitution granted the residual rights to states: education, family law, and most crimes etc. The Bill of Rights (enacted in the first ten Amendments) protected citizens' fundamental rights. An independent Supreme Court will keep other branches in check. It was a self-balancing act.

## THE PRESIDENT

An executive elected by the people could become tyrannical—so direct election was ruled out. The option for the legislature to appoint him was also rejected since that could make the legislature dictatorial.

So a cumbersome system of Electoral College (though the term is not used in the Constitution) was devised to elect the president. The composition of the Electoral College is somewhat peculiar. Each state chooses electors equal to the number of its representatives in Congress, i.e. two Senators plus the House representatives. Thus, the total number of electoral votes for all the states is equal to the number of representatives in Senate (100), plus the House (435, plus 3 for District of Columbia). That number is 538. The magic number to win the election is 270 electoral votes.

People in each state vote for the electors, not for the president; then electors vote usually for the winner, though they can break their pledge. What if the Electoral College is divided? In that event, the House of Representatives (12th Amendment) decides. The decennial census is now used to reapportion the number of electors among the States.

The Electoral College is not an exact proxy for popular votes. Gore, who had won the popular vote, found it out when George W. Bush won the 2000 elections. Despite severe voting irregularities in Florida, the US Supreme Court refused to allow a recount and declared Bush the winner. That decision disenfranchised the Gore majority. The Electoral College is an anti-democratic institution that drags on despite hundreds of proposals to eliminate it over the years.

The President is elected for four years with a limit of two terms—instituted after Franklin Roosevelt was elected four times.

## The Rise of a Strong Presidency

Despite the Framers reservations, the presidency has emerged as the strongest branch of the government. It was perhaps inevitable—no government can run without a leader. Rapid economic and social changes and vast territorial expansion of America demanded a focal point of policy and decision-making. A squabbling and an incompetent Congress was not fit for timely decision making. Now the President takes the initiative, introduces appropriate legislation and gets Congress to act—by persuasion, hand-shaking, and even bullying. The system was built on the assumption of debate and compromise in national interest. What if Congress refuses to pass the bills sent by President? This the Framers could not visualize. And this is exactly what's happening today. The result is the Washington gridlock.

## THE HOUSE OF REPRESENTATIVES

The Framers decided on electing the House every two years but did not limit the terms. House seats (435 now) are apportioned among the states by population. In a nation divided by partisan politics, the short two year term can disable a president to carry out his agenda—if his party loses majority in the House two years after his election. Obama lost the majority in 2010 elections. The short two-year election cycle without term limits has aggravated the role of money; the incumbents keep raising funds for the next election, fulfilling promises to the donors, and ignoring the voters.

All revenue bills originate in the House, though the Senate may propose or concur with amendments as on other bills. House Speaker is elected by the majority party, and is next in the line of presidential succession after the Vice-president.

## THE SENATE

The first question before the Convention was whether to have one chamber or two. Here too, the separation of powers doctrine and the English model influenced the outcome. Remarkably, both Thomas Paine and Franklin foresaw the deadlocks in future with two chambers and warned that the people's chamber was enough in a democracy. They lost. The Framers were enamored with their untested, abstract theory of the separation of powers, and their dream of a Senate dedicated to public good. They were also concerned with protecting the aristocracy from the demands of a poor and uneducated majority.

The Senate was the favorite child of the Framers. Coming from privileged families, they could see themselves sitting in Senate chambers, deliberating, passing measures for the public good. While the lowly House representative was given a two-year term, and the President four, the Senators were favored with a six year term—on top of no term limit. In 1913, the Seventeenth Amendment eliminated the election of Senators by State legislatures and allowed direct elections.

The Framers' intent was to allow the Senators time to wrestle with the nation's problems and come up with wise solutions. It turned out to be a huge mistake and a pipe dream. Now the Senators spend their time on dinner parties to raise funds, and building relationships with the capitalists. All these privileges have turned the Senate into an undemocratic body—it does not consider itself answerable to the nation or the people. It acts like a chamber of one hundred Marie Antoinettes.

## Is Senate Undemocratic?

One of the most hotly debated issue before the Convention was whether the Senate seats be allocated to a state on the basis of its population (proportional representation) or statehood.  The delegates of the "small states" were adamant on having an equal representation without regard to their population. To most delegates, including the highly respected John Madison, the surrender of the proportional representation in a nascent democracy was reprehensible. This led to contentious debates and a walk out by the small states. With the barrel of the gun in their face, the delegates blinked. Historian Forrest McDonald says: *"The conclusion seems inescapable that extraordinary means of persuasion had been applied to the North Carolina delegates (*to agree to this compromise*), but I shall not speculate here as to what those means might have been"* [Novus Ordo Seclorum, The Intellectual Origins of the Constitution (1985), 237]

Thus, now to say that everything the Framers did was well thought out or intended by them is plain wrong. They were just as susceptible to blackmail as most reasonable men are when confronted with a totally unreasonable child, partner, or political adversary.

Now look at the consequences of that decision. Since each state has two Senators without regard to its population, two senators from Wyoming represent less than half a million people, while the two senators from California represent 34 million. Today, the nine largest states with majority of Americans have only 18 seats (out of 100 senators) in the Senate. It raises the question: who is represented: the people or the acreage? Is such representation consistent with democracy? With the equal protection clause?

If there was little reason before, there is none now. America is a Union (as the Civil War established) and not a Confederation.

Furthermore, the composition of the Senate adversely affects the representation rights of racial and ethnic minorities because those minorities do not hold majorities in any state and are thus left out from any representation in the Senate.

## How the Majority Rule Has Been Turned into Minority Rule

Senate rules permit what is called 'filibuster' which allows a senator, or a series of senators, to speak for as long as they wish on any topic, unless a supermajority of three-fifths of the Senate (60 Senators) brings the debate to a close. In last two decades, the Senate has used this procedural rule to block all legislation unless the president's party has 60% majority in the Senate. The Constitution requires 51% majority to pass a bill. What happened to the mandate of the Constitution that the country would be ruled by "We, the People?"

Robert Dahl, a Constitutional Law professor at Yale, has discussed this in *How Democratic is American Constitution*? And Richard N. Rosenfeld (*What Democracy? The Case for Abolishing the Senate*, *Harpers*, May 2004) has argued that Senate was and continues to be an anti-democratic and irresponsible institution.

## Abuse of Power: Delaying Judicial Confirmations

The constitution requires Senate to confirm judicial appointments by the President. An obstructionist Senate can withhold these confirmations for political advantage. During President Bill Clinton's tenure, he nominated 24 people for 20 different federal appellate judgeships. Of these 20 seats in question, the Senate only filled four seats, and did not act on the rest. Fourteen were later filled with Republican nominees of GW Bush. Similarly, of the 42 federal district judgeship vacancies, 17 were filled with Clinton nominees, 24 by GW Bush. This abuse of power has now become a standard Republican 'tactic.'

This practice is a threat to the principle of judicial independence so dear to the Framers. By stacking judiciary with judges of its own ideology, the independence of the judiciary is being compromised, and turning the courts into kangaroo courts. The right-wing judges come with an agenda driven by ideology—not the nation's interest. If a time limitation had been provided in the Constitution for confirmation of judges, failing which the confirmation would be automatic, such an abuse of power could have been avoided.

In January 2012, when Senate would not confirm Richard Corday as Chief of Consumer Protection Agency because it did not want any Agency to protect the consumer, Obama sidestepped the Senate and made a recess appointment even though Senate was not in recess. Obama said, "...when Congress refuses to act and as a result hurts our economy and puts people at risk, I have an obligation as President to do what I can without them."

## THE SUPREME COURT

The Framers set up an independent judiciary by giving the judges life tenure—unless impeached, and separating them from the influence of legislature and the executive. Preoccupied with other matters, the Framers spent very little time on the Supreme Court. The Framers did not even debate whether the laws passed by Congress—representing the supreme will of the people should be allowed to be overturned by a few judges. In *Marbury v. Madison* [5 U.S 137 (1803)], the Court decided that it has the ultimate power to decide that. The fact that the Supreme Court is now deciding cases on partisan basis is profoundly changing American democracy.

## IS U.S A REPUBLIC OR A DEMOCRACY?

Based on their reading of the Greek political system, democracy to the Framers meant "mob rule." So they set up a republic, though they had no clear idea what a republic was, except that in a republic no one had hereditary status, and America was to be a representative democracy. John Adams considered public virtue to be essential to a republic. Madison thought it was a government in which the landed aristocracy, the wealthy class, checked the 'excesses' of the common people, and the hunger of an executive for power, as the House of Lords curbed the English King. If America was a Republic in the sense it was a federation of States, the Civil War established that it was a Union first and foremost.

Madison changed his views in 1834, and said the words 'republic' and 'democracy' were interchangeable. And Jefferson, who had created the Democratic-Republican Party, dropped the word "republican." Today, the distinction has no meaning. A number of countries in the world today called themselves democratic republics. To assert that America is not a democracy but a republic is misleading. This myth is fostered by the Republican party to create the impression that it truly represents the Constitution and the Republic, and that the Democrats represent the 'mob.'

## CRACKS IN THE CONSTITUTION

The Constitution's pivot was debate and compromise. The Separation of Powers required goodwill and cooperation between the President and Congress, and an independent Supreme Court. It

18

worked for two centuries because the nation came first to all the parties. But when one party began putting its interest first and representing the rich to the exclusion of the people, the system began to fail.

## Obsolescence

The Framers were mortals and fallible. They had not seen the working of any democracy. Since 1787, over 120 countries have adopted democracy. Christianity was the only religion then, now America is a multi-cultural nation. America's population has grown from 3 million to 330 million. The country was isolated then, now it is a superpower. The procedure for amending the Constitution has been rendered difficult because the number of states has gone up from 13 to 50.

Remarkably, no other country has adopted the American model because it does not provide for accountability. In fact, it encourages irresponsibility.

## The English Model is Dead

The separation of powers was based on the British model which the Framers greatly admired. That model has long since been consigned to the dustbin of history in deference to the people's need for accountability. In 1911, the House of Lords (the Senate counterpart) was stripped of its power to veto legislation sent by the House of Commons. Lords can delay by one year but not veto the legislation. The chief executive (Prime Minister) in UK, and other democracies, has to deliver on his party's agenda disclosed during the election. He delivers on the agenda as the leader of the majority party in the House of Commons which passes the necessary legislation.

Contrast this with the plight of the US President. The President has to ask both the House and the Senate. Though leader of his party, he does not control the party; the party discipline is loose. His own party members often vote against him. And if the Congress is determined to deny his every request, there is little he can do. More often than not, it is the Senate that refuses to work with the President. The Senate is now a feudal institution that has not changed since 1787.

In America, the Constitution is sacred—the foundation and the symbol of America's meteoric rise. It is ironic that the British— sticklers for traditions—summarily changed the House of Lords when it became a hindrance to the people's will. America—with no regard for traditions— continues to cling to it. We seem to forget that a ship that would take us to farther shores is any day preferable to the Titanic.

## Lack of Accountability

The separation of powers has created a system in which neither the President nor the Congress is accountable. And this irresponsibility has been exacerbated by the Supreme Court's descent into party politics. To get votes, the parties bait the public with misinformation and lies and a phony agenda. The public is sedated by speeches, party conventions, creative ads and the barrage of well-orchestrated attacks on the opponents. It is like a soap-opera. The elections have become a form of public entertainment. This circus goes on for over a year. The public ends up paying a huge price in the end.

Once the Republican party wins the election, it switches to its real agenda: huge tax cuts for the rich, and reckless spending to 'defund' the safety-net. Reagan and GW Bush promised fiscal responsibility, and then went on to bankrupt the treasury. Yet the voters overlooked the Republican fiscal record in the 2004 election; they were more focused on GW Bush's 'born-again' religion, and how impressive he looked in the debates.

The fixed four-year term of President adds to lack of accountability. A president with a secret agenda, and a majority in Congress, can deliver to his patrons. While a four year term is too little for building a nation, it is enough to destroy it. GW Bush proved it by increasing the country's debt by about 8 trillion. During his tenure, he hid behind lies, his cronies, and controlled press conferences. He declared Iraq war because he saw "mushroom clouds." What option do the people have? They can keep wringing their hands and wait for his term to end. The provision for impeachment, for all practical purposes, is as good as non-existent.

In parliamentary democracies like England, Bush would have been thrown out in six months. It is this fear of being dumped on the street that makes the British Prime Minister act with sanity and restraint.

## Frequency of Elections and Lack of Term Limits

The House members are elected every two years, and so are 1/3 of the Senate members (who have a six year term). There are no term limits. This feature, along with the primaries, has greatly contributed to the elected officials' irresponsibility to the electorate. The need for fund-raising is relentless; the members have turned into year round fund-raising machines. Fraternizing with and working for the donors, they corral the electorate with words.

## SEPARATION OF POWERS HAS BEEN TURNED INTO TYRANNY

In the minds of the Framers, only the separation of powers could save the people from the tyranny of government. And it did work for a long time. Since 1980, however, the GOP has figured out a way out to turn this shield into sword with the magic wand of ideology.

Here is how it works: if the President and the Congress share the same ideology, then there is no separation of powers between the executive and legislative branches. And if the majority (five out of nine justices) in the Supreme Court also shares the same ideology, and the three branches are pursuing the same agenda, there is absolutely no separation of powers. That's how the communist and fascist regimes pursue the same agenda at all governmental levels. And that's exactly what is happening in America. Example: When a Republican President proposes to raise the debt-ceiling, and the Congress keeps raising the debt-ceiling without asking questions, there is no separation of powers. And if the Supreme Court's five Republican justices uphold an anti-environment law on ideological ground, the separation of powers is dead. During 2001-2006, there was no protection—either from the Congress or from the Supreme Court because the majority in Congress and on the Supreme Court had the same ideology as the President. This ideological unity among the three branches of government is a perfect set up for tyranny. It happened in *Citizens United v. Federal Election Commission* [558 U.S. 08-205, (2010)] in which the Supreme Court struck down campaign finance reform law on ideological grounds: the Republican party is opposed to any campaign finance reform. Such tyranny is the direct result of the irresponsibility created in the first place by the separation of powers. And this has been going on since the time of Reagan. In a court of nine justices, five make the majority. GW Bush's won in 2000 elections largely as a result of the rightwing majority in the Supreme Court which stopped the vote counting in Florida and handed over the

22

Presidency to Bush. It is for this reason that GOP uses every tactic to delay confirmation of judges in the Senate, and to load the courts with rightwing justices. When Rehnquist and O'Connor left, GW Bush appointed Samuel Anthony Alito and Justice Roberts to Supreme Court—both Republican conservatives, and member of the Federalist Society. With five Republican justices on the Supreme Court, the Court has consistently decided cases along party-ideology lines. "We, the people" referred to in the Constitution got a double whammy—first no accountability—and now tyranny.

# III

## DUMP LINCOLN!

## AND DIVIDE THE HOUSE:

## A BRIEF HISTORY OF THE PARTIES

*An honest politician is one who, when bought, will stay bought.*-Simon Cameron, Republican Boss of Pennsylvania (1860)

Amerca is a paradise for the political parties: Power without responsibility. Where else can one find it? The Republican party faithful live in the hind quarters of Eden—flush with cash—and guard the gates of their gods' mansions with an automatic rifle in hand, and a big sign hanging around their neck: NO TAX SOLICITATION HERE. Occasionally, when they get lucky, their get to shine their shoes.

### HISTORICAL BACKGROUND

Democracy is not monarchy, dictatorship or theocracy. In those forms of government there is no accountability to the people. The relationship between the people and the party in power in a democracy is similar to that between an investor and his financial trustee. The trustee of assets cannot play fast and loose with his client's assets, gamble with them, or apply unproven theories to invest them. Madoff did it and will spend the rest of his life in jail. So why has the Republican party not paid any price for its fiscal irresponsibility to the nation? Because a political party in

American democracy can get away with it. As long as the public does not notice.

The Framers considered the political parties to be mischievous if not downright evil. George Washington contemptuously called them "factions." Yet, before the ink had dried on the Constitution, two parties had emerged. On one side were the Federalists like Alexander Hamilton and John Adams, who believed in a strong national government, on the other side were anti-federalists like Jefferson who believed in minimal government. In his later years, Madison came to favor political parties and the majority rule. Before 1820, the parties nominated a single candidate from their party for the President's job.

In the hotly contested presidential election of 1824, Andrew Jackson won the popular vote but not enough electoral votes (recall Gore v. Bush in 2000). The House of Representatives chose John Quincy Adams the president. Outraged, the Jacksonians formed the Democratic Party, and Jackson won in 1828. The defeated politicians who opposed Jackson formed the Whig Party. From 1832 the nomination was done by a national convention where political bosses controlled the delegates.

Over the next few decades, slavery emerged as the single most important issue that divided the parties. The Republican Party was born around 1850s out of both Democrats and northern Whigs who called for abolition of slavery on moral grounds. It nominated Lincoln who won the election. The Civil war showed that a national party had to preserve the ideals of American independence, democracy and the Constitution. These values put the Republican party on top for next several decades; the Democrats became a party of a special interest group—the slave-owners in South—for which they dearly paid.

In 1896 election, Democrats attempted to regain lost ground but William McKinley, a Republican, won the business and the urban vote. He followed conservative fiscal policies and in 1900 committed the US currency to Gold Standard. He expanded presidential powers on the ground that only the president represented the nation in the US government. The U.S. economy improved during his administration, and the Republican Party earned the label "the Grand Old Party (GOP)."

McKinley was succeeded in 1901 by Theodore Roosevelt. Now the U.S. had become a fully industrialized nation. Dynamic and ambitious, Theodore Roosevelt invited Booker T. Washington, a prominent black civil rights activist, to dinner in the White House just after a month of taking over the office. Fearing destruction of wilderness by private interest groups, he established five National Parks for future generations, and kept an eye on business excesses. When he decided to prosecute the Northern Securities Company for violations of the Sherman Anti-Trust Act, the Detroit Free Press commented, "Wall Street is paralyzed at the thought that a President of the United States should sink so low as to enforce the law." He passed the first legislation to regulate the meat packing industry whose sickening practices were portrayed by Sinclair in his book *The Jungle*. It was a time when the Party had a moral bone.

## WHAT LED TO THE 1929 DEPRESSION

The U.S. got involved in World War I during the eight years the Democrats were in power. The Republicans returned to the White House in 1920 with Warren Harding. Recovering from the trauma of war, Harding decided to restore America to "normalcy" which to him meant golf, poker and extra-marital affairs. Calvin Coolidge, the next Republican president, liked Harding's style of presidency. Against the warning of his advisors, he spent a lot of time getting photographed in amusing and diverse poses and costumes and admiring himself in the mirror. His self-indulgent style of presidency allowed the bankers to play fast and loose with financial regulations. The result was a runaway capitalism and the stock market crash in 1929. When unemployment soared, Herbert Hoover, the next Republican president, had the commonsense to coin the term 'Depression' but not the intellect to handle it.

## DEMOCRATS IN THE DRIVER'S SEAT

The Democrats won the 1932 election; Franklin Roosevelt was the man of the hour. With a legislative package of relief and reform for the masses called the "New Deal," he brought relief to the unemployed and poor, empowered labor unions, and enacted Social Security legislation. He put the economy on the recovery path by economic stimulus, and reform of the financial system. He stabilized the banking system and persuaded the public to take out their cash from under the mattress and deposit it in the reopened banks. He viewed government's role as the key to economic regeneration. The New Deal coalition (1936–1968) included, among others, workers, labor unions, Catholics, Jews, and racial minorities. His reforms formed the backbone of Democrat's success in the mid-twentieth century. But to some capitalists, the New Deal was an enemy of business and growth—regardless of all the evidence to the contrary.

Economic recession spread to Europe. It allowed demagogues like Hitler and Mussolini to seize dictatorial power, and unleash World War II. Ironically, the war brought Depression to an end in the U.S and revitalized the economy. The combination of Depression at home, and the war in Europe and the Pacific, led to Roosevelt's election four times. The law was later changed to limit the Presidency to two terms. Henry Luce, the founder of *Time*, and

*Life,* said that 20th century was "The American Century," in which, in the words of Roosevelt, America recognized that it had a "rendezvous with destiny." By the time he died in 1945, Roosevelt had taken his place alongside Lincoln and put Democrats in the driver's seat for decades to come.

Harry Truman (1945-54) was the first President to televise his address from the White House. General Eisenhower (1953-61), the war hero, won on the Republican ticket after Truman, and left the New Deal largely intact. In the 1960s, communism was seen as a real threat. At a time when McCarthyism was sweeping America, several capitalists in the U.S. became engaged in clandestine anti-communist activities through several "front" organizations that were supported by the CIA. Eisenhower took a pragmatic view of the world and warned against the take-over of America by the military-industrial complex. One of Eisenhower's major achievements was the construction of the interstate highway system which ushered in the age of the new middle class, automobile, and the suburbia.

The Civil Rights movement became a live issue when the blacks won an important victory in *Brown v. Board of Education* (1954) which ended racial segregation in schools. In 1960, the young and charismatic John F. Kennedy, a Democrat, caught the pulse of times in his inaugural address: *...Let the word go forth from this time and place...that the torch has been passed to a new generation of Americans..."* He foresaw that the explosive nature of civil rights movement, and warned: *United there is little we cannot do...Divided there is little we can do.* His promise was cut short by an assassin in 1963. He was succeeded by Lyndon Johnson.

The 1960s was a time of great social upheaval in America. The children of World War II generation revolted against the old establishment which they saw as form over substance. Martin Luther King's "I have a Dream" speech energized the Civil Rights movement, the birth pill became the catalyst for women's freedom, occupation of Alcatraz island symbolized Native Americans uprising against their ill treatment, and the white ethnic offspring of the "new immigration," galvanized the Latino population. The New Left launched an environmental movement. But it was the Vietnam War that brought all under one tent; colleges and universities became hotbeds of war protests and a "countercultural" life style was born—free bed-hopping, rock, drugs, jeans, tea-shirts, radical politics and ethnic pluralism. It left the old generation feeling lost.

Lyndon Johnson (1963-69) came with a vision of America as the "Great Society"— putting an end to poverty and racial injustice that had plagued America for two centuries. He took Roosevelt's New Deal policies further by passing the Civil Rights Act in 1964 that ended discrimination on the basis of race, religion, and national origin. His Medicare and Medicaid measures extended health insurance provision for the elderly and those on low incomes. The Civil Rights Act was the most far-reaching legislation since Reconstruction after the Civil War. It was a continuation of Lincoln's vision of the country as one nation.

In the presidential election in 1964, Johnson won a landslide victory over the conservative Republican candidate Barry Goldwater and signed the Voting Rights Act in 1965, another landmark legislation that enfranchised the blacks for the first time in the nations' history. Various community-action agencies were established that gave the poor a voice in housing, health, and education programs. In 1965, Congress also abolished the discriminatory 1924 national-origin immigration quotas thus triggering a new wave of immigration from South and East Asia and Latin America.

## GOP RIDES ON THE PASSIONS INFLAMED BY CIVIL RIGHTS

One hundred years after Lincoln's death, the nation was still not ready for racial integration. In 1958, four years after the *Brown v. Board of Education*\* decision, Jerry Falwell thundered from his Church pulpit,"… The facilities should be separate. When God has drawn a line of distinction, we should not attempt to cross that line." He attacked Martin Luther King in 1964 as a Communist. Thousands of segregationist schools were established in the South to avoid racial integration. Falwell himself opened one school. He later complained, "In some states it's easier to open a massage parlor than to open a Christian school." [\*347 US 483].

Inflamed by the Civil Rights measure, the Democrat Governor George Wallace (Alabama) defected from the party and ran as an independent in the 1968 presidential election. Until now, the whites in South had been solid democrats, but all that changed. This shift enabled Republican Richard Nixon to score a narrow victory in 1968 and win overwhelmingly in 1972. A new racial realignment of voters was taking place.

The Republican strategists like Paul Weyrich and several others wasted no time in exploiting the opportunity. They approached the wealthy conservatives with a proposal to win the South by spreading a new and a radical religion with the gospel of privatization. They calculated that the conservative Christians would fall for a radical doctrine. To these new initiates looking for funds from the rich, Bible doctrine was a great vehicle for spearheading the cult of unbridled capitalism. In 1973, with generous funding from Joseph Coors, the beer baron, and Richard Mellon Scaife, a newspaper magnate, Paul Weyrich and Ed Feulner founded the Heritage Foundation as a think tank to oppose prevailing views on taxes and business regulation. In 1974, with money flowing from the conservative rich, Weyrich started what later became the *Free Congress Foundation* (FCF) to attack "multi-

31

culturalism, judicial activism, and democratic politicians," on grounds of "moral decay." This group included, among others, Richard Viguerie, a small advertising and publishing company owner, Howard Phillips, founder of *The Conservative Caucus* (TCC), and Ed McAteer, a sales manager for Colgate-Palmolive with the glib tongue of his profession, who believed that marketing Jesus was no different than marketing soap. By 1978, Paul Weyrich's Political Action Committee (PAC) had swept into Congress a new, radical breed of populist conservatives. Weyrich had harvested what his friend Morton Blackwell (founder of the *Leadership Institute* in 1979), termed "the greatest track of virgin timber on the political landscape: evangelicals." Appeals to fear and loathing amongst Christians and raising funds by mail was the brainchild of Richard Viguerie who raised millions for conservative causes.

In 1979 Ed McAteer founded the *Religious Roundtable* of 56—a forerunner of the *Council for National Policy* (CNP), created in 1981—to back the candidacy of Ronald Reagan and to politicize millions who believed in "traditional, family-based Christian values." The *Religious Roundtable* was a coalition of conservative business, military, political, and religious leaders. The list of board of directors and early members of the *Religious Roundtable* reads like Who's Who of the future CNP.

In 1979, McAteer invited Rev. Jerry Falwell to meet these leaders who built the Moral Majority. Rev. Falwell pledged to "turn this (country) into a Christian nation." Joseph Coors generously funded the *Moral Majority*; he also helped to build the headquarters of organizations such as the Heritage Foundation and Free Congress Foundation (FCF). According to Sara Diamond in *Spiritual Warfare: The Politics of the Christian Right:* " About this time, Weyrich proposed that if the Republican Party could be persuaded to take a firm stance on its 1980 platform against abortion, that would split the strong Catholic voting bloc within the Democratic Party." He was right. Their agenda influenced the GOP party platform in the 1980 election and laid the foundation of GOP's strategy of dividing the country to win elections.

This group had close connections with Rev. Sun Myung Moon. Terry Dolan, co-founder and national chairman of the 300,000-member *National Conservative Political Action Committee* (NCPAC) was a former member of the advisory board of Moon's political organization—CAUSA. In 1984, Dolan's organization, NCPAC, received $775,000 from Rev. Moon. Terry Dolan stated that the secret of fundraising is to try to "make them angry and stir up hostilities. The shriller you are, the easier it is to raise funds. That's the nature of the beast."

## Why the Capitalists Fomented the New Right?

The opportunity of controlling the Republican political party to get what they want was too good to pass. These men—Nelson Bunker Hunt, the Texas oil billionaire, Joseph Coors, the beer baron, J. Peter Grace, the shipping magnate (and chairman of the Order of the *Knights of Malta*), the Koch brothers of Koch Industries (one of the largest oil company group), Fred Koch (one of the founders of *John Birch Society)*, and Richard Mellon-Scaife, the newspaper magnate—had been opposed to Roosevelt's New Deal, and Johnson's Great Society. They called it communism or socialism to take advantage of anti-communist public feelings at the time. It was good propaganda. After World War II, they had been active in supporting anti-communist activities alongside the CIA, especially in Latin America and Central America. Funding for the U.S. branch of the World Anti-Communist League (WACL)—*U S Council for World Freedom* (USWCF)—came from Joseph Coors and Texas oil billionaires Hunt brothers. They were familiar with conspiracies, covert operations, and creation of "front" organizations to incite local 'insurgent' groups--with funds, arms, and supplies. Some belonged to *John Birch Society*—an anti-communist, anti-socialist political advocacy group—that viewed the US Constitution as based on Christian principles.

These men had a sense of entitlement to their wealth not unlike the welfare recipients whom they vehemently denounced. They did not want to pay taxes; they did not want business regulations. They did not believe that the American democratic society—with its high standard of living, good education, cutting edge technology, a skilled workforce, and good infrastructure--was the generator of their inherited wealth. They were no entrepreneurs, innovators or creators of wealth like Steve Jobs, Bill Gates or Warren Buffet who knew that an egalitarian society is essential for creation of wealth through competition and hard work. They wanted to thwart competition by the advantages of wealth. In the Republicans they found a party eager to insure their inherited wealth by low taxes, no estate taxes, and minimal business regulations in exchange for financial support. The Party made a deal with Mephistopheles by giving away the soul of America.

Rev. Moon of Korea, a self-proclaimed messiah, a foreigner, was looking to buy political influence. He had the financial support of Sasakawa, a billionaire and a Japanese WW II war criminal. Once convicted for tax fraud, Moon founded *CAUSA*, an anti-communist organization that sponsored conferences for evangelical and fundamentalist Christian leaders and for US Senate staffers and conservative activists. His money bought him Reagan's friendship, and he went on to advance the cause of Religious Right by founding *The Washington Times* in 1982 (a year after Reagan victory) for which he spent over $1 billion. He also helped Reagan in his clandestine Contra-war efforts. In 1987, Moon sent hundreds of Church demonstrators to Berlin asking the Soviet leaders to bring down the Berlin Wall. Criticizing gay rights in

1997, Moon said, "What is the meaning of lesbians and homosexuals? That is the place where all different kinds of dung collect. We have to end that behavior."

**The Moral Majority:** Moral Majority burst onto the political scene in 1979 with Jerry Falwell's trumpet call: "get them saved, get them baptized, and get them registered." The New Right savaged Carter all through the 1980 election campaign, assailing his manhood, his judgment, his nerve. Thousands of fundamentalist preachers participated in political training seminars that year and by June 1980, more than two million Christian voters had been registered Republican. Their goal was to register five million by November. Sensing the significance of the Moral Majority to his election, Reagan appointed Rev. Robert Billings, the Moral Majority's first executive director, the religious advisor to his campaign. In the 1980 elections, the newly politicized Religious Right succeeded in unseating five of the most liberal Democrats in the Senate, and provided the margin that put Ronald Reagan over Jimmy Carter. Later, Reagan appointed Billings to a position in the Department of Education.

With their man installed in the White House, Falwell, Weyrich, Edwin Meese, and Pat Robertson started to work on their plan of solidifying the Right. In the annual Family Forum national conferences, leaders of Christian Right groups and activists rubbed shoulders with members of the Reagan Administration. Feulner, President of Heritage Foundation— an ironic and misleading title since the *Foundation* was out to destroy America's heritage of egalitarian society—served on the Executive Committee of the Reagan's Presidential Transition. *The* Heritage Foundation guided the Reagan administration during the period of its transition; Joe Coors sat on the President's "Kitchen Cabinet." During its first year, the administration adopted fully two-thirds of the recommendations of *Heritage's Mandate for Leadership: Policy Management in a Conservative Administration*. These included:

rollback of minority programs, dramatic increase in military spending, and drastically cutting taxes of the rich. In 1984, *Heritage* published *"Mandate for Leadership II"* for Reagan's second term. It recommended privatization of Social Security and denial of special educational funding for the handicapped. See Bellant, Russ, *The Coors Connection.* John Saloma's *Ominous Politics: The New Conservative Labyrinth* (1984), referred to *Heritage* as a "shadow government" of Reagan. Under the influence of the Heritage Foundation and CNP, Reagan commenced an era of reckless deficits to "defund" the democratic social programs— Social Security and Medicare, public education—to strengthen the Religious Right by destroying the Democrat voter base.

Soon after Reagan's victory, the Council for National Policy (CNP) was formed (See Chapter Six) in 1981 as a one stop shopping resource for the Right. It brought leading conservative religious and political leaders, financiers and activists together under one roof. While *Heritage* developed and sold the Religious Right ideology in the cloak of 'public policy' to policy makers, CNP's role was to strategize, and fund cash-generated "grassroots" movements, controversies, and issues that would promote the Religious Right. CNP won Reagan's full support in raising money for its anti-communist Central America policies. It even got the President embroiled in the Iran-Contra Affair scandal.

**Was Reagan a Religious Fanatic**? One should stop and ask: did Reagan really believe in the extreme Religious Right positions: low taxes, little business regulations, anti-abortion, anti-gay, high military expenditures, and huge deficits. Did Reagan have fanatic tendencies in his character? In his growing up years and up to middle age—when he worked in films, radio, and the army—he was a liberal democrat, opposed to racial discrimination; he admired Franklin Roosevelt and the New Deal. In 1954, at 43, he was hired by General Electric (GE) to give conservative, pro-business speeches and appear on television. Lacking his own beliefs based on independent thinking, in 1962 he joined the Republican party as a fiscally conservative but otherwise a liberal Republican. As Governor of California, he was pro-choice and liberalized abortion laws, passed no-fault divorce law, and raised taxes to their highest level in California's history to create a budget surplus.

**What Changed Reagan?**   He had come in office with the help of die-hard rightwing ideological men who knew how to manipulate human psyche to achieve their goals. In Reagan they found a man who had no personal beliefs.  Reagan readily embraced their cause: he lowered taxes for the rich, spent recklessly, and incurred huge national debt—raising the debt-ceiling for the highest number of times (18) among the U.S. presidents. He had promoted abortions in California, now he vehemently opposed abortion.  He had been a fiscal conservative, now he became fiscally reckless. He advanced a movement whose goal was to divide the nation for political power. Apparently, he let these men lead him; he did not lead. Among others, he fathered the birth of several organizations that today are at the forefront of pro-Wall Street, anti-democratic movement: the *CNP*, the *Federalist Society*, the *Washington Times*, *Americans for Tax Reform* (the one that makes elected Republicans sign a no-tax-increase pledge). Roger Ailes, president of Fox News, was media consultant for Reagan's election campaign. Reagan also started the process of politicizing the Supreme Court—so important to the Religious Right—and began stacking the judiciary with activist rightwing judges. In his election campaign, he promised "to appoint only those opposed to abortion and the 'judicial activism' of the Warren and Burger Courts." Reagan even nominated—without success—Robert Bork, who wanted to roll back civil rights decisions of the Warren and Burger courts. What changed him so radically? Ambition? Lack of principles? A blank mind?

## THE RISE OF AN AGGRESSIVE RELIGIOUS RIGHT

There are at least 80 million evangelical Christians in the United States attending more than 200,000 evangelical churches. This caught Rev. Pat Robertson's eye. He founded Christian Coalition in 1989 as a tax-exempt IRC Sec. 501(c)(3) non-profit religious organization. It had two goals: to control the agenda of the Republican party, and to train and elect pro-family values Christian candidates to public office. In 1988 he ran for the Oval Office because, he said, he was endorsed by Highest Authority (the same that urged GW Bush to run for Office). Though he lost to Bush Senior, the race generated a mailing list of 3 million evangelical Christians, whose rage he transformed into the *Christian Coalition* against the establishment.

Pat Robertson laid out key organizing principle in his book *The Millennium*: "With the apathy (among the voters) that exists today, a well-organized minority can influence the selection of candidates to an astonishing degree." Robertson hired Ralph Reed as the *Coalition's* political mastermind. To get the Christian Right candidates elected, Reed and Robertson taught them to use stealth: avoid publicity, stay out of debates, and work below the radar screen. Don't call attention to yourself. Ralph Reed told a *Coalition* gathering, "The first strategy, and in many ways the most important strategy, for evangelicals is secrecy." At one time he boasted, "*I want to be invisible. I do guerrilla warfare. I paint my face and travel at night. You don't know it's over until you're in a body bag. You don't know until election night.*"

While rightwing candidates avoided the limelight, Christian Coalition "Family Values Non-Partisan Voter Guides" were quietly distributed to thousands of participating churches endorsing Republican candidates. Church telephone directories were used for "get-out-the-vote" telephone banks. By election time in 1994, Christian Coalition had distributed 40 million copies of the "Family Values Voter's Guide" in more than 100,000 churches nationwide. As a result, the Republicans took control of Congress in 1994 for the first time in 40 years—also called the "Newt Gingrich Revolution."

The victory reaffirmed the Republican's belief that their party's only chance for regaining political hegemony was by demonizing the opposition and by converting the political arena into a battleground between "godly Republicans" and "secular, anti-religious" "liberal" Democrats. Out of forty-five new members in the U.S. House of Representatives and nine in the U.S. Senate in 1994, roughly half were Christian Coalition candidates. It was also the year that Republicans made huge gains in state legislatures.

In 2000, 75 million voter guides were sent out to support George Bush. Eighty-four percent of evangelicals voted for Bush, providing nearly one-third of his total votes. After all these years, what had looked like a dream to the evangelicals, and to the puppeteers behind the show, it had become a reality when GW Bush was elected. Christian Coalition changed the course of American politics with the landing of its loose cannon in the White House.

The Christian Coalition was sued by the Election Commission for coordinating its activities with Republican candidates for office in 1990, 1992 and 1994 and failing to report its expenditures. It lost its tax-exempt status in 1999 and Robertson left it in 2001. But the candidates elected by the *Coalition*'s illegal activities and fraud are still out there.

What about Pat Robertson's own morality? Far from the media's gaze, Robertson used the tax-exempt, nonprofit Operation Blessing (Revenues—$407 million annually) as a front for his shadowy financial schemes, while exerting his influence within the GOP to hide his tracks. In 1994, he made an emotional plea on *The 700 Club*, one of his organizations, for cash donations to support airlifts of refugees from the Rwandan civil war to Zaire (now Congo). Reporter Bill Sizemore of *The Virginian Pilot* later discovered that Operation Blessing's planes were transporting diamond-mining equipment for the African Development Corporation, a Robertson-owned venture initiated with the cooperation of Zaire's then-dictator Mobutu Sese Seko. After a protracted investigation, Virginia's Office of Consumer Affairs determined that Robertson "willfully induced contributions from the public through the use of misleading statements and other implications." Yet when the time came in 1999 to prosecute Robertson, Attorney General Mark Earley, a Republican, overruled prosecution but agreed that Robertson had deceived the public. Two years earlier, while Virginia's investigation was gathering steam, Robertson had contributed $35,000 to Earley's campaign—Earley's largest. Against this 'high' bar of moral standard, the Republicans' condemn Democrats' "moral decadence."

In 1997, Christian Broadcast Network (CBN), Robertson's ministry, took in $164m in donations plus an additional $34m in other income. The tidal wave of tax-deductible cash generated by this daily dose of 'holiness' paid for the cable channel which was sold in 1997 to Rupert Murdoch of Fox News, along with the old sitcoms that filled the remaining broadcast hours, for a cool $1.82 billion. Christian writers such as Cal Thomas have also blasted Robertson over his race horses and gambling. He has used, it is alleged, the lists of donors to his tax-exempt religious charity to promote a network marketing operation under the name 'Kalo-Vita', selling vitamins and other items. His book, *The New World Order*, was the 1991 bestseller that the *Wall Street Journal* described as written by *'a paranoid pinhead with a deep distrust of democracy.'* His message that Jesus came to make us wealthy, as played out on *the 700 Club*, is diametrically opposed to what Jesus preached. But this appeals greatly to tens of millions of desperate people looking for a quick financial salvation. One of Robertson's former business partners who often travelled in the minister's jet, recalled that he never saw Robertson crack open a Bible. 'Everywhere we were flying he had the *Wall Street Journal* and *Investors' Daily*.' It was all about making money and growing the client list (church membership) so the pastor can make more money. On February 4, 2010, at his war crimes trial in Hague, Charles Taylor, the Liberian president, testified that Robertson had volunteered to make Liberia's case before U.S. officials in exchange for gold mining concessions granted to Robertson's *Freedom Gold Ltd* corporation. Pat Robertson's net worth is over $500 million, Rick Warren's over $200 million, Joel Osteen's over $50 million and on and on it goes. And these pastors strut on the stage ranting and raving about sin to millions of rapt Christians on television.

Ralph Reed, the mastermind behind the Christian Coalition, fell from grace after a year of steady revelations about his ties to the convicted former GOP super lobbyist Jack Abramoff, who charged $85 million in lobbying fees from Indian tribes by various fraudulent but ingenious schemes. Abramoff amassed a fortune by showering gifts on Congressional and executive branch officials in the Bush administration. He worked with Reed to close the Tigua tribe casino, then persuaded the tribe to hire him to lobby Congress to reopen the casino. In emails made public, Abramoff repeatedly referred to Native Americans as "monkeys", "troglodytes" and "morons." He was jailed (after his release, he took a job at Tov Pizza in Baltimore, Md). Grover Norquist of Americans for Tax Reform, a billionaire-appointed messiah of "no tax increases," was also involved in funneling the tainted money. *"This is sleaze of a high order,"* commented the *New York Times* on March 22, 2005.

## RELIGIOUS RIGHT'S CROWNING ACHIEVEMENT: THE BUSH VICTORY

The Religious Right candidates are now in the U.S. Congress, state legislatures, the courts, state boards of education and more. Almost all of them want to abolish the IRS and most of the taxes. Tom DeLay, the ex-House Speaker, thought he was the king of the Dominionists—the theocracy of Religious Right. Following the re-election of GW Bush and a new generation of conservative lawmakers nationwide, Jerry Falwell launched a new organization, *The Faith and Values Coalition*, as the 21st Century Moral Majority. On the significance of the role of old Moral Majority (which was disbanded in late 80s), Jerry Falwell commented, "Many historians believe the result was the election of Ronald Reagan in 1980 and the genesis of what the media calls the "Religious Right."

When former Senator John Danforth (R-MO), who is also an Episcopal priest, wrote an OP-ED to the *New York Times*, March 30, 2005, criticizing the Religious Right for its extremism, Weyrich's response was telling:

*Without the "values voters," the Republicans couldn't get elected dogcatcher*, he said, then added: *Do you want to return to the way it was before the religious right became part of the GOP coalition? If that happens, the Republican Party will be dead. Its majorities in both the House and Senate soon would evaporate and the party would be unable to elect a President.*

The evidence of Right's success is everywhere. The so called "liberal" press has been squashed by Fox News and Sun Myung Moon's *Washington Times*, and Dominionists talk show hosts spew their right wing political venom from coast to coast. Currently, it is estimated  fewer than 100 U.S. commercial radio stations carry liberal talk programs, compared to around 600 stations for Rush

Limbaugh, 500 for Sean Hannity—and there are several more. Gay marriage and abortion are touted as "moral issues" and "family values" to attract the "values voters." For them, destroying the economy and the environment at home, and denying healthcare to millions of children are not "moral" issues. Morality has been turned on its head.

Rob Boston in *United Americans for Separation of Church and State* feature "Religious Right Rebound" noted in May 2011 that "Three years after being pronounced 'dead' by many pundits, fundamentalists are riding high in Washington and many state legislatures. Social issues are suddenly all the rage again. Bolstered by legions of Tea Party activists who exploited fears over unemployment rate and a shaky economic outlook, conservatives swept to victory in November 2010…De-funding Planned Parenthood has been a long-sought Religious Right goal and Tea Party has revived it as a deficit-cutting measure. At this point, the connection between the Religious Right and the Tea Party has become clear. A February 2011 analysis by the *Pew Forum on Religion & Public Life* found that 89 percent of Tea Party supporters said they agreed with the agenda of the Religious Right. The Religious Right organizations collectively raise nearly $1 billion every year, and are now a permanent fixture on the American political scene. Its secret is in taking full advantage of the good times during Reagan and GW Bush years. The Democrat presidents have been unable to do anything because the Democrats' financial base has been decimated by the Republicans.

# IV

## THE IDEOLOGY:

## JESUS LOVES GUNS AND THE RICH

*We have just enough religion to make us hate, but not (enough) to make us love one another.* –Jonathan Swift: Thoughts on Various Subjects

◎

I n this book, the terms Religious Right, Christian Right, the New Right or just the Right have been interchangeably used. The Religious Right ideology is known as Dominionism or Reconstructionism. It calls for a theocratic government in America. It states that Christians have a mandate from God to occupy the political institutions, based on Genesis 1:26:   *"Then God said, 'Let us make man in our image, in our likeness and let them rule over the fish of the sea and the birds of the air, over the livestock, over all the earth and over all the creatures that move along the ground.'*

It overlooks John 18: 36:  Jesus said, *"My kingdom is not of this world."* And Mark 12:13-17: And Jesus said, *"Render unto Caesar the things that are Caesar's, and to God the things that are God's..."* And Matthew 17:24-27: Peter answered, *"Yes, Jesus pays the tax."*

### THE AGENDA

The Religious Right agenda includes *all* of the following:

1. **The Capitalists Agenda.** A "free market" economy—low taxes, small government, no business regulations, and privatization of

education, healthcare and government agencies, and break all trade unions.

2. **The Republican Party Agenda.** Win Congress, the White House, and fill the Supreme Court and other courts with rightwing judges. De-fund the Democratic "safety net"—New Deal, Medicare, and Social Security to ensure power.

3. **The Theocratic Agenda.** Enact laws based on Bible. Eliminate separation between Church and State.

The Christian Right has, strangely, embraced the capitalists' special agenda of free markets. "Most taxes are unbiblical," according to Beliles and McDowell, authors of the textbook *America's Providential History* in their chapter *on Christian Economics.* "Income tax is "idolatry," property tax is "theft" and estate taxes are simply not allowed in the Bible." It views the death penalty as "the backbone of civil government."

Leaders of the Reconstructionism advocate:

"... death penalty be used to punish those guilty of 'apostasy (abandonment of the faith), heresy, blasphemy, witchcraft, astrology, adultery, 'sodomy or homosexuality,' striking a parent, incorrigible juvenile delinquency, and in the case of women, 'unchastity before marriage.' Non-capital crimes would be sanctioned with whipping, indentured servitude, or slavery.

Journalist Katherine Yurica has pointed out on her blog that the best way to understand the Religious Right is to look at the kinds of legislation their lawmakers have sponsored in the U.S. Congress and in state legislatures: anti-women, anti-labor, and anti-civil rights, anti-campaign finance reform, anti-environmental protection; pro-gun; and opposed to: social justice for the poor, public education, healthcare, theory of evolution, human sexuality.

## THE STRATEGY

**Step One**: Capture Congress and the White House. Fill the courts with rightwing judges.

**Step Two**: Whenever in power, defund the Democratic "Safety Net' programs by incurring huge deficits and giving large tax cuts to the rich. This is also called "starve the beast" strategy.

**Step Three**: Eliminate freedom of religion until most of America is converted to Christianity.

To build his earthly kingdom, Rick Warren, the author of the bestselling *The Purpose Driven Life*, calls himself a "stealth evangelist." He plans marketplace ministries—business ventures with a veneer of missionary 'compassion' (GW Bush style)— that would slip into a country in order to transform it systematically through the governmental, corporate, and social sectors.

## THE TACTICS

It is in its tactics that the Right's hatred for democracy is unmasked. Dominionism takes the view that America has descended into a humanist society which threatens Christianity. God's people have a moral duty to bring down this 'godless' government. Apply these to Republican politics as you read.

The Religious Right's tactics were laid down in *the Free Congress Foundation (FCF)*'s strategic plan on how to gain control of the U. S. Government (by Eric Heubeck in 2001), in *"The Integration of Theory and Practice: A Program for the New Traditionalist Movement,"* and dubbed as Paul Weyrich's *Teaching Manual* (hereafter the *Manual*). The *Manual* has of late been removed from the *FCF*'s website for obvious reasons. The excerpts here are published at the *Yurica Report*.

- 1. Falsehoods are not only acceptable, they are a necessity. The corollary is: The masses will accept any lie if it is spoken with vigor, energy and dedication.
- 2. It is necessary to be cast under the cloak of "goodness" whereas all opponents and their ideas must be cast as "evil."
- 3. Complete destruction of every opponent must be accomplished through unrelenting personal attacks.
- 4. The creation of the appearance of overwhelming power and brutality is necessary in order to destroy the will of opponents to launch opposition of any kind.
- 5. "We must," Weyrich once suggested, "develop a network of parallel cultural Institutions existing side-by-side with the dominant leftist cultural institutions...(for) the development of a highly motivated elite...designed to make an impact, and change the character of American popular culture."
- 6. "Our movement will be entirely destructive, and entirely constructive. We will not try to reform the existing institutions. We only intend to weaken them, and eventually destroy them. We will endeavor to knock our opponent's off-balance and unsettle them at every opportunity. We will maintain a constant barrage of criticism against the Left. We will attack the very legitimacy of the Left. We will not give them a moment's rest. We will endeavor to prove that the Left does not deserve to hold sway over the heart and mind of a single American. We will offer constant reminders that there is an alternative, there

is a better way...The rejection of the existing society by the people will thus be accomplished by pushing them and pulling them simultaneously..."

- 7. "We will use guerrilla tactics to undermine the legitimacy of the dominant regime...We must be feared, so that they will think twice before opening their mouths.
- 8. "We will be results-oriented rather than good intentions-oriented...*We must reframe this struggle as a moral struggle, as a transcendent struggle, as a struggle between good and evil*..." (Emphasis theirs).

## A COMPARISON WITH WAR TACTICS

Weyrich's tactics closely resemble war tactics laid down in Robert Greene's *The 33 Strategies of War* (2001): strive relentlessly toward your goal; hit your enemy where it hurts (i.e. defunding); hide your motives and wage a dirty war—use deception, feed misinformation, and lies; transform your war into a moral crusade, create an atmosphere of fighting for something noble, a cause or a need to demoralize the enemy, use the polarity strategy to divide and conquer, maintain constant pressure to defeat enemy's will power; use command-and-control strategy—have a bigger plan (See Chapter Six). It is no accident that Green's book is a recommended reading at *Southwestern Baptist Theological Seminary* course in *Christian Apologetics.*

Have Republicans been on a war-path against the people?

## THE RELIGIOUS RIGHT'S FOUNDING FATHER: MACHIAVELLI

Dominionism is the antithesis of Christianity. How did it come about? What inspired it? Machiavelli. Leo Strauss, a Jewish scholar who fled Hitler's Germany and later taught at the University of Chicago, resurrected Machiavelli and became the father of the neoconservative movement. In his book, *American Dynasty*, Kevin Phillips tells us that Karl Rove, former Bush political strategist, is a devotee of Machiavelli, and so was GW Bush. Strauss' influence extends to Pat Robertson, Justice Thomas, Robert Bork, Irving Kristol and his son William, Alan Keyes and many more.

Strauss upholds the necessity of a religion—not because he favored religious practices—for a ruler to control the population. *Any religion will do for this purpose.* This characteristic of religion enabled the Religious Right to create a Machiavellian religion—a mish-mash of economic-political -religion. Nobody questions a religion because it is religion. Machiavelli advises: *"Let a prince therefore aim at conquering and maintaining the state, and the means will always be judged honorable and praised by everyone, for the vulgar is always taken by appearances."*

Religion also keeps revolt in check; it is the free thinking humanists that rebel. But religion alone may not be enough. Strauss also believed that to have a stable political order, a foreign threat is essential to unite the people. Following Machiavelli, Strauss maintained that if no external threat existed, then one ought to be manufactured.

Does this explain the Iraq war? Little comfort to the dead! But it did win Bush a second term.

Michael Ledeen and Harry Jaffa, two better known students of Strauss, throw more light on Machiavellian tactics. Ledeen believed "the end justifies the means." The idea is that the leader does evil to achieve good result. What is "good?" What the ruler believes to be good is good. This finds a resonance in the Christian doctrine that Christians can use evil to bring about good. Hence it's fine to kill an abortion-clinic doctor. William O. Beeman, a journalist, wrote in the *Pacific News Services*: *Ledeen's ideas are repeated daily by such figures as Richard Cheney, Donald Rumsfeld and Paul Wolfowitz; and Karl Rove often consulted Ledeen.*

## MACHIAVELLI AND THE U.S. CONSTITUTION

Harry Jaffa (Professor Emeritus at Claremont McKenna College), a conservative, had close connections with Dominionists like Pat Robertson, and influenced Robertson's views on how to interpret the Constitution. Jaffa did not accept the view that the Constitution was secular or a social contract. Jaffa believes that the *Declaration of Independence* was the premier document that superseded the Constitution: "The Declaration...is the charter of the nation. It is what you might call the articles of incorporation, whereas the Constitution is the bylaws. The Constitution is the means by which to carry out the great purposes that are articulated in the Declaration." Jaffa's thinking influenced Clarence Thomas, Antonin Scalia, and Edwin Meese III, who founded the *Federalist Society* (See Chapter 7) to assist in the implementation of the Right's agenda.

In an interview with Jaffa in 1986, Robertson asked, "The principles enunciated in the *Declaration of Independence*, how far have we gone from it and what can we do to redress some of these problems?" Jaffa responded cryptically: "I'd say that today, for example in the Attorney General's [Edwin Meese's] warfare with the liberals on the Supreme Court, in his appeal to original intent, he appeals to the text of the Constitution. Jefferson and Madison said together in 1825, '*If you want to find the principles of the Constitution of the United States, you go first to the Declaration of Independence.*'" By the term "original intent" Jaffa meant that the Constitution must be interpreted according to what it meant when it was originally adopted.

Jaffa went on: *The Declaration of Independence* says *"whenever any form of government becomes destructive of these ends [life, liberty, and the pursuit of happiness], it is the right of the people to alter or abolish it, and to institute new government, laying its foundations on such principles and organizing its powers in such form, as to them shall seem most likely to affect their safety and happiness."*

The foregoing statement seems to authorize a minority to impose its will on the majority as long as the majority lacks the will to resist the minority. Falsehood succeeds if it is not exposed. This Machiavellian approach explains the secretive nature and the aggression of the Religious Right.

However, *The Prince* was written in the 15th century for kings and despots when monarchy was the only form of government; Machiavelli had never heard about democracy or the majority rule. For a political party in a democracy to use secrecy and deceit so that its rich clients--a small minority--can rule over the masses by brainwashing them would seem like a conspiracy against the people.

Shadia Drury in *Leo Strauss and the American Right* (St. Martin's Press, 1999) points out that "rightness of their ends" is just a façade to seize power and perpetuate it. Under this approach, Nixon would be justified in authorizing the Watergate "break-in," Reagan in selling arms to Iran, and GW Bush in orchestrating lies and deception to invade Iraq. Every ruler believes in the rightness of his ends or propagates that illusion. And it often works—for a while. Look at Lenin, Hitler, and Mussolini. What is remarkable is that the public does find out about a "leader's" ideology but then it is too late.

# V

## THE PROPAGANDA MACHINE:

## SMOKE AND MIRROR ORGANIZATIONS

*The most curious social convention of the great age in which we live is...that religious opinions should be respected.*—H.L. Mencken: American Mercury

⓪

Right network organizations mushroomed during the late 1970s and early 80s to expand the Republican voter base. A whole new field was opened by the 'family values' propaganda. As if people had been living until now without family values! But the purpose of these 'family values' was to create controversy, divide the electorate, and get independent votes.

In the 20th century, ideologies were used by Lenin, Hitler, Mussolini, Stalin, and Mao to seize power. All ideologies are crafted to appeal to the people and delivered by a well-heeled propaganda machine. Facts are ignored; misinformation is fed by creating a frenzy of "us versus them" in the media. This misinformation is endlessly repeated in the "echo-chambers"--the 'mantra' of all ideologies. All rational thinking is numbed.

Many vote Republican despite the uneasy feeling their vote was against their own economic interest: they can ill afford the soaring costs of privatized education, private healthcare, and loss of Social Security and Medicare. But emotions are more powerful—hence profitable for exploitation by manipulators. These tactics have won the Republicans elections in 1980, 1984, 1994, 2000, 2002, and 2004. Then again in 2010, the Trojan horse was slipped into the Tea Party—the 2010 election Republican victories stopped the Democrats in their track.

## DIVIDE AND CONQUER: THE IMPERIALIST FORMULA IN A DEMOCRACY

The Party in past had relied on support of the gun lobby, flag-waving "patriots," believers in a militarily strong America, but above all, in fiscal conservatism. But fiscal conservatism did not give the Republican party political dominance. Hence fiscal conservatism was abandoned in favor of the new "free market" ideology which favored the rich and hurt the masses. It could only be sold by resorting to deception. So a propaganda machine was created. The strategy has succeeded. While all groups in the country other than the rich have suffered, the Republicans have won the White House seven times in the last forty years and lost only four times including the 2008 election.

The rich—the Coors family, Koch brothers, the Hunt family, Richard Scaife family, and several other likeminded capitalists-- funded the propaganda machine and had the strategy developed with the help of anti-government activists, church pastors, Republican "strategists," and fascists.

The term 'free-market' as used by the rich has little in common with the free-market theory of Nobel Laureates Milton Friedman and Friedrich August van Hayek. The term has been hijacked by them to mislead. It means: lower taxes, business deregulation, privatization of public schools, privatization of healthcare, squashing labor unions, and killing pro-environment laws. Small government is a euphemism for dismantling the "safety net": Social Security, Medicare, and privatization of all public programs including the post office and prisons. It means rolling back American capitalism to the one that was in vogue in the 18th century England—whose ills Charles Dickens exposed so vividly in his novels.

Let us take a look at the relationship between tax cuts and government spending. Taxes constitute revenues for government to fund defense and public services. Similarly, tax cuts are regarded as (tax) expenditures by economists. Yet, the "free market" version of the crony capitalism puts it differently: tax cuts are 'economic stimulus' (investment)—not expenditure--that grows the economy and creates jobs, while "safety net" programs are expenditures that increase the national debt and amount to communism or socialism because they lead to "radical redistribution of wealth." In the minds of the rich, "redistribution of wealth" to the rich through lower taxes is good for the economy. This has been the Republican party's ideology since Reagan came to office.

The following list of organizations is partial. The purpose is to give the reader an idea of the breadth and the reach of the Religious Right.

**Factors Common to the Entities**

- Funded by the billionaires.
- Deceptive names: Americans for Prosperity; Americans for Tax Reform; Traditional Values Coalition; Concerned Women for America; The Family Research Council; American Family Association; Focus on the Family; Heritage Foundation, etc. The names appeal to emotions and hide the real purpose. This is the classic Trojan horse strategy—what's hidden is lethal, what's visible is innocuous and sweet.

- They beat the drum of 'morality' to mislead the 'low-information' voters. Gay rights and abortion are the prime targets. The moral issues are picked and emphasized based on public polls.
- They are invariably set up as 'non-partisan' tax-exempt 501(c)(3) organizations—religious or educational—so they pay no taxes on income, and allow donors to take tax deduction. Partisan political activity, especially for candidates can result in loss of tax exemption. Undeterred, they all lobby for the Republican candidates. Having political support in high places, many openly flout the law. One example: When *Americans United for Separation of Church and State* filed a complaint in the 1990s with the IRS against *Second Baptist Church* in Houston, Texas, for alleged partisan political activity, right wing leaders went ballistic. In his television show, "The 700 Club" on *Christian Broadcasting Network* (CBN), Pat Robertson accused *Americans United*'s Barry Lynn of "taking the fascist position" of muzzling the free speech right of religious groups. Robertson called church-state separation a "myth" and a "lie of the left." Jay Sekulow, then head of *the American Center for Law and Justice (ACLJ)*, a Pat Robertson Christian legal advocacy group, warned the IRS in a letter, "... the IRS better not become the pawn of *Americans United*..."

The journal *Humanist* (Jan.-Feb. 2011) reports that the IRS is failing to enforce this provision, even as some pastors openly defy the law by holding annual "Pulpit Freedom" events in which they deliver explicitly political sermons. "If houses of worship were allowed to engage freely in partisan political activity," The *Humanist* wrote, "*Americans United* foresees the day when a large church or a group of churches working together could form a political machine that dominates a community's political life."

## TYPES OF ORGANIZATIONS

It should be noted that the categories are only for simplification and often overlap.

## POLITICAL- RELIGIOUS

Mega churches have sprung up across America—like shopping malls, large corporate campuses, universities, and sports arenas—since 1970s. Their number is over 1,300 today—up from just 50 in 1970. They have huge stages, rock bands, jumbotron screens, and bring in over $8.5 billion a year. Combined, these new "electronic churches" in 1980s drew weekly audiences of almost 20 million viewers and turned a lot of pastors into multi-millionaires. Many pastors became bestselling authors of Christian books which were distributed through a network of Christian distribution channels. Christianity is a flourishing industry—thanks to Republicans. The few below are among the better known. But new and bigger ones keep coming. When desire for fame and money overtakes religion, it is not greed. It is salvation.

**Pat Robertson Empire**: Robertson, a Dominionist, media mogul, TV evangelist, ex-Baptist minister, and businessman, has founded numerous organizations: the Christian Broadcasting Network (CBN), the Christian Coalition (dissolved in 2001), the Regent University, the American Center for Law and Justice (ACLJ), a public interest law firm to defend First Amendment rights of Christians. These organizations have annual budget of hundreds of millions. Robertson has been a governing member of the Council for National Policy (CNP).

**Jerry Falwell Empire:** Jerry Falwell was an evangelical fundamentalist Southern Baptist pastor, televangelist, and the leader of "Moral Majority"—one of the largest political lobby groups for evangelical Christians in the 1980s which is credited with delivering the Reagan victory in 1980.

After his death in 2007, his empire is now run by his two sons. It includes Liberty University (Budget: $396 million) which has experienced huge growth and now has an active online learning site. Despite Falwell's anti-government rhetoric, Liberty students receive nearly half a billion dollars in federal aid every year.

**Focus on the Family** (FOF): Founded by child psychologist James Dobson, host of the radio show, Focus on the Family, it advocates "biblical" solutions to family problems with a budget of over $130 million. Opposed to church-state separation and secular government, the massive fundamentalist ministry has a worldwide presence. It has a network of "family policy councils" in 35 states that lobby in state capitals. James Dobson founded the *Family Research Council* (FRC) in 1983 to act as the political lobbying arm of his radio show. An estimated four million listeners daily tune into his radio show. FRC seeks to merge fundamentalist Christianity with US government. It opposes female reproductive freedom, engages in gay bashing, and lately has sought to join forces with the Tea Party to create a massive, far-right phalanx.

**Free Congress Foundation** (FCF): Founded by Paul Weyrich, it received the startup money from the Coors family, and Richard Mellon Scaife. Russ Bellant, a New Right researcher, indicated that by 1988 Scaife had donated over seven millions to it. FCF worked to redefine the Catholic Church's policies. It had a convicted Nazi collaborator on its staff, Laszlo Pasztor, who came to the U.S. in the 1950s and joined the GOP's ethnic unit. He was forced to resign from the 1988 Bush campaign when his past came to light. (See Russ Bellant, *Old Nazis, the New Right and the Republican Party*,

South End Press (1999). One section of the FCF (Center for Law and Democracy) lobbied for the appointment of conservatives judges to the federal courts, another worked on building conservative institutions and "defunding" liberal institutions.

*"Are we on the verge of a second American Revolution? In the old Soviet Union, the government seemed all-powerful–until one day it came tumbling down,"* Weyrich wrote in 1986 in an article in *The Washington Post* and **recommended a new Constitution and form of government for the U.S.**

**American Coalition for Traditional Values**:  Founded by Rev. Timothy LaHaye, the best-selling author of  the *'Left Behind'* series which sold in millions, it was funded with over 5 million dollars of Rev. Moon's money. [ See, http://watch.pair.com/moon.html]   It had 110,000 churches committed to getting Christian candidates elected to office.

**American Family Association** (AFA): Founded in 1977, it is a fundamentalist Christian lobbyist group. According to the AFA website, the group has "has launched a national campaign to place before our children a copy of the official motto of the United States: "In God We Trust" and centrality of God in the life of our republic." In 1990, it established the *AFA Center for Law & Policy* as a litigation and public policy arm to defend any lawsuits by the ACLU free of charge. It has underwritten a series of "pastor policy briefings" in various states to organize fundamentalist churches into a political machine. It claims to own and operate nearly 200 radio stations across the country.

**Alliance Defense Fund** (ADF): Formed by a group of TV and radio preachers in 1993, it was a funding pool for organizations to promote theocratic views and undermine church-state separation. It engages in direct litigation and has a network of sympathetic attorneys nationwide. It attacks public education and opposes legal abortion and gay rights. It sponsors "Pulpit Freedom Sunday," a ploy to openly defy federal tax law by encouraging pastors to endorse or oppose candidates from the pulpit. While claiming to be nonpartisan, all the participating clergy in 2008 openly endorsed Republican John McCain and opposed Barack Obama.

**Southern Baptist Convention Ethics & Religious Liberty Commission:** It is the lobbying arm of the Southern Baptist Convention (SBC), the nation's largest Protestant denomination. SBC claims 16 million members. The SBC's government action office presses for school-sponsored religion, tax aid to religious schools, reductions in gay rights, limits on legal abortion and other far-right social issues. Although many Baptists had historically supported church-state separation, in the early 1980s it was taken over by fundamentalists.

**Concerned Women for America** (CWA): Founded in 1979 by Tim LaHaye and his wife Beverly, it was formed to counter the women's rights movement. It claims 500,000 members. Under Reagan's influence in 1980s, it launched a special project to attack Nicaragua's Sandinista government. The group focuses mainly on opposing abortion, gay rights and "secular humanism" in public education. Lately, CWA has been adding fiscal issues to its agenda like reduced government spending. Its current targets include Planned Parenthood, the National Endowment for the Arts, Public Broadcasting and NPR.

## THE INCUBATOR THINK TANKS

**The Heritage Foundation:** The *Foundation's* influence on Reagan had established its clout. Renovated in 2002, *Heritage's* new office space includes intern and fellow apartments, a 200-seat auditorium, a private fitness center, and two floors dedicated to expanding the research department.

In the 1980s, Rev. Moon was looking to buy influence in the Reagan administration. So South Korean intelligence covertly donated $2.2 million to the *Heritage Foundation.* Heritage's president, Ed Feulner, took an active role in promoting South Korean issues in Congress. In 1977, it employed Roger Pearson, a British race scientist, who was the head of the World Anti-Communist League (WACL), a multinational network of Nazi war criminals, Latin American death squads and North American neo-fascists. In 1975, Pearson organized the U.S branch of WACL—*Council on American Affairs.* Paul Weyrich's *Free Congress Foundation* provided office space for Laszlo Pasztor, a convicted Austrian pro-Nazi collaborator. Weyrich was greatly influenced by Nazi tactics and Nazi propaganda machine. Viewed as Weyrich's right hand man, Pasztor's *Coalitions of the Americas* was a subsidiary of *Free Congress Foundation,* the political arm of *Heritage Foundation*, which received over seven million from the Scaife Foundations. Throughout the 1980s, *Heritage* framed the Reagan agenda relating to armed conflicts in Nicaragua, Afghanistan, Angola, Cambodia and El Salvador.

The resources of the *Foundation* were responsible for Newt Gingrich's 1994 revolution: *Contract with America. Heritage* has served as a breeding ground for many neo-conservatives. The positions developed by it are used by executives, legislators, journalists, governors to bolster right-wing actions. *Heritage* supports faith-based initiatives, school vouchers, ban on abortion, and anti-affirmative action programs. Apart from its pivotal role in Reagan administration, it takes credit for much of President GW Bush's policy, both domestic and foreign, referring to Bush's policies as "straight out of the Heritage play book." It published *"Priorities for the President,"* and also wrote "A Budget for America" for the Bush administration. At least five key appointments in Bush's first term went to *Heritage* former employees. Bush set aside $300 million dollars for states and local communities to "promote marriage." Since the Reagan era, the *Foundation* has advocated controversial weapons programs like missile defense, large defense budgets, and a hawkish line against potential U.S adversaries, and favored an expansive "war on terror." It has spawned many organizations that are working to privatize government agencies. And Justice Thomas's family has received large sums from *Heritage Foundation*.

**The Cato Institute:** A libertarian think tank and a neo-conservative organization, the *Cato Institute* supports: privatizing Social Security, abolishing minimum wage, abolishing affirmative action, and abolishing most environmental regulations. Charles Koch, the billionaire co-owner of Koch Industries known for its financing of the Tea Party and various extreme right front groups, is the chairman. Even Rupert Murdoch had a place on the board at one point. According to the *Center for Public Integrity*, between 1986 and 1993 the Koch family gave eleven million dollars to the *Institute*. Today, *Cato* has more than a hundred full-time employees, and its experts and policy papers are widely quoted by the mainstream media. It has consistently pushed for corporate tax cuts, reductions in social services, and laissez-faire environmental policies, privatization of healthcare and Social Security.

**The American Enterprise Institute** (AEI): According to its website, AEI has six divisions for policy research:: Economic Policy, Foreign and Defense, Health Policy, Legal and Constitutional Studies, Political and Public Opinion Studies, and Social and Cultural Studies. Former Vice President Dick Cheney has been on AEI's board of trustees. A 2006 *Washington Post* article described AEI as "a think tank that has had strong influence in staffing the [Bush] administration and shaping its ideas."

**National Center for Policy Analysis** (NCPA): Established and funded by wealthy conservatives, including Charles and David Koch and Sarah Scaife Foundation, it is a dedicated to providing private sector and free-market alternatives to government regulated institutions. It aggressively targets key political leaders and special interest groups, establishes on-going ties with media, and testifies before Congress, federal agencies, state lawmakers, and national organizations.

**National Center for Privatization** (NCP): Willard Garvey and other Kansas businessmen founded the NCP In 1983 (the name has since been changed to Council for Government Reform) to accelerate the process of eliminating government by representation. After leasing the federal lands at low rates, the group turned around and subleased it at much higher rates, pocketing the difference. In *Waste of the West: Public Lands Ranching,* (Chapter 7), author Lynn Jacobs describes Willard Garvey's illegal use of tax-funded public lands: "with a little help from fellow rancher, Ronald Reagan, who also happened to be President of the United States."

In 1984, appraisers for both the Bureau of Land Management (BLM) and Forest Service uncovered more than 2000 secret subleasing deals that provided the original holder of the grazing permit 'the opportunity to profit at the expense of the Treasury.' That was the real reason for the push toward privatization.

On 6 April 1984, Garvey wrote to President Reagan, "...Privatization is documented in the enclosed paper from the *Heritage Foundation* and dates back at least to Adam Smith, Plato, Aristotle and Jesus...Privatization is essential for national salvation." His salvation! See,

[http://watch.pair.com/cnp.html#ncp]

**Discovery Institute:** It's a non-profit public policy think-tank best known for its advocacy of intelligent design creationism in school curriculum. Howard Ahmanson, Jr. is the major funder.

## LOBBYING AND CAMPAIGNING

**The National Conservative Political Action Committee** (NCPAC): Founded in 1975, it led the charge for conservative Republicans in the 1980s, including the election of Ronald Reagan as President. To circumvent campaign finance restrictions on political action committees, it used an organization to pool independent contributions that spent on campaign attack ads. Chairman Terry Dolan was quoted as saying, "A group like ours could lie through its teeth, and the candidate it helps stays clean." It opened a new era in sleaze politics.

**Americans for Prosperity** (AFP): It is a political advocacy 501(c)(4) organization, and the political action arm of *Americans for Prosperity Foundation* (AFPF), a tax-exempt organization. It is run by Koch brothers—David and Charles— who own a group of companies involved in refining and chemicals. AFP supports "cutting taxes and government spending in order to halt the encroachment of government in the economic lives of citizens..." *AFP* has worked to defeat both smoke-free workplace laws and cigarette excise tax increases. It is opposed to pro-environment legislation. AFP acts as a political barrier to a clean national energy policy. The Koch brothers spent $37.9 million from 2006 to 2009 for direct lobbying on oil and energy issues—only ExxonMobil ($87.8 million) and Chevron Corporation ($50 million) spent more. More than 600 lawmakers and candidates, primarily

Republicans, have signed a pledge to oppose pro-environment legislation. Can such practice be viewed as buying the legislators?

During the 1990s, Koch Industry pipelines were responsible for more than 300 oil and chemical spills in five states, which prompted the Environmental Protection Agency (EPA) to impose a penalty of $35 million. Before the 2000 presidential elections, their company faced a 97-count federal indictment for concealing illegal release of 91 metric tons of benzene, a known carcinogen, from its refinery in Corpus Christi, Texas, and 350 million dollars in fines. Under GW Bush, the Justice Department dropped 88 of the charges. Two days before the trial, John Ashcroft, the Attorney General, settled for a plea bargain in which the company pled guilty to falsifying documents. All major charges were dropped, and Koch and Ashcroft settled the lawsuit for a fraction of that amount.

AFP has 23 state chapters and was a major supporter of Republican candidates in the 2010 elections, a year in which its budget grew to $40 million from $7 million in 2007. AFP tapped Herman Cain, the ousted 9-9-9 presidential primaries candidate, as the public face of its "Prosperity Expansion Project" in 2005 and 2006 to establish AFP chapters, preaching the ills of big government. Cain continues to work with AFP operatives.

AFP encourages conservative activists to develop strategies to counter left-wing bloggers and develop conservative New Media techniques. The Koch PAC donated directly to 62 of the 87 members of the 2010 House GOP freshman class, and to 13 governors that won in 2010. The Koch brothers have pledged to raise $88 million for the 2012 election. AFP is active in stopping Wall Street reform, and is opposed to all election finance reform.

The Koch brothers have ties to The John Birch Society of which their father was a founding member, and several other conservative think tanks and organizations including the Heritage Foundation, the American Legislative Exchange Council (ALEC), and the Cato Institute. The John Birch Society follows the model of Communist cells and quasi-secret operations through "front" groups, and believes in a ruthless prosecution of the ideological war along Nazi and Communist lines.

AFP created an offshoot "front" group called Patients United Now, which organized hundreds of rallies to bulldoze the health-care reform. The Koch brothers whipped up the Tax Day Tea Party protests on April 15, 2009 and have been funding the "grassroots" Tea Party movement. David Axelrod, Obama's senior adviser, said, "What they don't say is that, in part, this is a grassroots citizens' movement brought to you by a bunch of oil billionaires."

A video on YouTube (on February 26, 2011) shows Hagerstrom, the director of AFP Michigan, advocating "*taking unions out at the knees so they don't have the resources*" to fight for workplace benefits or political candidates. Between 1997 and 2008, the Koch brothers collectively gave more than $17 million to groups lobbying against unions.

AFP was also behind Governor Scott Walker's budget and labor-law initiatives. When those initiatives were opposed in 2011 in Madison, Wisconsin, it backed and led counter-protests. According to *Politico*, in August 2011 AFP sent misleading ballots to Democratic voters with instructions to return the ballot before August 11, 2011--the last date for the election was August 9.

The Democratic Congressional Campaign Committee filed a complaint against the AFP, a 501(c)(4) organization, for running political advertisements in violation of their tax-exempt status. AFP told the IRS in a 2011 tax form that it does not spend revenues on political activities. See,

[http://www.sourcewatch.org/index.php?title=Americans_for_Prosperity]

**The FreedomWorks**: An allied AFP organization, it is headed by Dick Armey, the former Republican Majority Leader. It promotes Social Security privatization. Working closely with Koch brothers, FreedomWorks helped to create the Tea Party, and opposed health care reform. It was largely responsible for hatred, paranoia and anti-government sentiments displayed at town halls during the health care debate. AFP has shown that money works—not freedom.

**American Crossroads**: A 527 organization, it is a "super" political action committee (PAC) associated with Carl Rove and the Kochs. There are no limits on contributions to 527s or on the donor; however, they must register with the IRS, disclose the donors and file periodic reports of contributions and expenditures. Its mission is to defeat Obama in 2012—it was very active in the 2010 U.S. midterm elections. It is the political arm of Crossroads Grassroots Policy Strategies *(Crossroads GPS)*, a 501(c)(4) nonprofit corporation, that works in conjunction with *American Crossroads.* For tax-exemption purposes, Crossroads *GPS's* states that its primary goal is the "advancement of social welfare including public policy advocacy." *Crossroads* GPS began running radio advertisements after 2010 elections urging members of Congress to prevent tax hikes.

*The Washington Post* reported on Dec. 3, 2010 that *American Crossroads* raised nearly $28 million, and the sister group GPS $43 million for a total of over $70 million from financiers, oil tycoons and wealthy individuals to influence the 2010 House and Senate races. And they did succeed. Republicans picked up more than 60 seats in the House to regain control. Total spending on the midterm elections was about $4 billion, including more than $400 million by independent groups.

The propaganda by the Tea Party focused on the national debt created by Obama administration to distract the public from the 2008 economic meltdown which resulted from the Republican policy of billions in tax cuts, uncontrolled spending, and bank deregulation under GW Bush. See,

[http://www.newyorker.com/reporting/2010/08/30/100830fa_fact_mayer#ixzz1UICr1m00]

**The US Chamber Of Commerce**:  *The Citizens United* allowed corporations to make political contributions just like the individuals. This fired up the *Chamber*. Representing big corporations, the *Chamber* received and spent more than $50 million in 2010 elections against health care and Wall Street reform. It opposes all laws designed to protect the American worker. After the election, Thomas Donohue, its head, said, American voters resoundingly rejected "more government spending, higher taxes, and more burdensome regulations that have caused crippling uncertainty for businesses."

**Americans for Tax Reform** (ATR): Run by Grover Norquist, it's best known for its "Taxpayer Protection Pledge." Candidates for federal and state legislatures are asked to sign in writing a pledge to oppose all tax increases or face defeat in next election. In the current Congress, 235 congressmen and 41 senators have signed the pledge; only seven Republican congressmen have not. ATR is another one of Reagan's contribution to divide America; it was founded in the mid-80s inside the Reagan White House. Norquist has said, "My goal is to cut government in half in twenty-five years, to get it down to the size where we can drown it in the bathtub." The debt reduction deal Congress passed in August, 2011 contained $2.4 trillion in spending cuts—and not a penny in tax increases sought by Obama. ATR has reduced Congress's power to tax to a farce.

ATR has also taken lead in other causes such as opposing campaign finance reform, permanently ending the "Death Tax," privatizing Social Security, and drastically increasing defense spending. ATR supported John G. Roberts' nomination to the Supreme Court. Norquist has led the Religious Right's charge to "de-fund" the left, declaring that *"We will hunt [these liberal groups] down one by one and extinguish their funding sources."* Norquist had close ties to GW Bush, and pushed for huge tax cuts.

ATR has several projects under its wings one of which is the Ronald Reagan Legacy Project. Its aim is to turn Reagan into a "great" President by naming airports and public buildings after him. But what would it do about Reagan's record?

**American Legislative Exchange Council** (ALEC):   ALEC sells a 'make-your-own-law' kit to big corporations. It has thousands of Republican state legislators as members who pay a nominal fee, while each corporate member pays an annual fee ranging between $7,000 and $25,000 a year.   The corporations get access to the legislators, who are wined and dined at corporate retreats.

 Then the real business begins. Legislators meet in closed back rooms and legislation is crafted by corporate lobbyists and their lawyers. Legislators then quietly introduce the bills.  The result is a pipeline of special interest legislation. ALEC boasts that it has over 1,000 of these bills introduced by legislative members every year, and one in five gets enacted into law.

More than 200 corporations including Coors, Scaife's Family and Allegheny Foundation, Amway, IBM, Ford, Philip Morris, Exxon, Texaco and Shell Oil and recently British Petroleum, have made contributions to ALEC when they get in trouble or need some law changed in their favor.

*"Corporations can implement their agendas very effectively using ALEC,"* says Edwin Bender of the National Institute on Money in State Politics.

ALEC also receives direct grants from corporations, such as $1.4 million from ExxonMobil during 1998-2009. It has also received grants from some of the biggest foundations funded by corporate CEOs in America, such as Charles G. Koch Foundation, the Koch-managed Claude R. Lambe Foundation, the Scaife family Allegheny Foundation, the Coors family Castle Rock Foundation.

ALEC's People-Grinder has been used for:

Tobacco industry against the smokers;

Oil companies against climate change proposals;

Pharmaceutical industry against less expensive prescription drugs;

Telecoms against municipality-owned cheaper or free broadband;

Insurance companies against responsible accounting standards;

Big banks against seniors on Medicaid;

Asbestos industry against people suffering from mesothelioma and other asbestos-related diseases;

Health insurance companies against healthcare reform.

ALEC helped Enron in deregulating the utility industry, which caused thousands to lose their pensions, and what the SEC estimated as $5 trillion loss in market value.

And yet ALEC is a tax-exempt organization. Because Republicans would not pay tax. That's what power means to them.

ALEC has also propounded bills to undermine organized labor by stripping public employees of collective bargaining rights. It's agenda is the agenda of the rich—to roll back laws regarding corporate accountability, workers compensation, job protection, collective bargaining rights, and the minimum wage rate. Another target is public education. Despite constitutional problems, negative impacts on public schools, bias against disadvantaged students, and comprehensive studies in cities like Washington DC, New York, Milwaukee, and Cleveland that have demonstrated that private school voucher programs has failed, ALEC continues to promote vouchers under the guise of "school choice," "Parental Choice Scholarship Act" and the "Education Enterprise Act." ALEC's goal is privatization, including the prisons. Privatization has been called "handing over public assets to cronies" for dimes.

With an eye on 2012 elections, ALEC has been recently spearheading an effort to enact voter ID laws in Republican controlled states to disenfranchise students and seniors, the illiterate and poor, Latinos, the blacks—the Democrat voters. It is done under the pretext of avoiding "voter fraud."

## THE MEDIA

Weyrich recognized early on that public ignorance could be manipulated into fear and hatred by spreading misinformation to build a political power base. The repetition of same views day in and day out begins to sound like truth. The other method to subvert truth is the 'stealth' politicking—the well-funded, carefully orchestrated "grassroots" movements.

GOP has created a highly vocal, an all compassing media organization: a $2.5 billion per year religious broadcasting industry, a slew of independent Christian book publishing companies, regional monthly newspapers, state-based think tanks that do legislative lobbying, and an array of legal firms devoted exclusively to advance Christian Right causes. This includes: the Fox News, the *Washington Times*, the TV and Radio Talk Show hosts. the Christian Right organizations of Pat Robertson and Jerry Falwell, and hundreds of other pastors who thunder down the conservative political agenda on their Mega- TV ministries. Talk show hosts—the likes of Rush Limbaugh and Glen Beck (now not on Fox)—skillfully rouse hatred and fear against certain targeted groups like the gays and the abortion clinics.

Fox News: Roger Eugene Ailes is the president of Fox News Channel. He was a media consultant for Republican presidents Richard Nixon, Ronald Reagan, and George H. W. Bush. Day in and day out, Fox News slanders Democrats, lies to the public, and supports conservative groups, activists and politicians. With its passion for lies, Fox News calls misinformation 'fair and balanced' news.

Roger Ailes, the Fox Chairman, is said to have advised Judith Reagan, a News Corp subsidiary (Harper and Collins) executive, to lie to federal investigators. She taped the conversation. When she did not lie, she was dismissed. She sued for wrongful termination, and within two months, a confidential settlement (2007) was reached. Fox paid $10.75 million to keep the truth from being disclosed. Truth is expensive! But lying is profitable. That is the model Fox and its talk show hosts have to live up to. Having Republicans in power is good for business.

## SOME OTHER ORGANIZATIONS

**Christian Right Media:** It is a group of TV and radio stations dedicated to fill airwaves with the Religious Right propaganda. It includes: Christian Broadcasting Network (budget: $295+ millions), Christian Examiner, Coral Ridge Ministries, Covenant News.com, Insight Magazine, Liberty Channel, Presbyterian Layman, Salem Communications, Ten Commandments News, Washington Times, World magazine, World Net Daily.

**Townhall.com:** Dedicated to conservative politics, it is a web-based publication, owned and operated by Salem Communications. It features more than 80 syndicated and exclusive columns by writers such as Jack Bouroudjian, Neal Boortz, Ann Coulter, Dinesh D'Souza, Larry Elder, Thomas Sowell, Jacob Sullum, Matt Lewis, Amanda Carpenter, Fred Thompson, Jeb Bush.

## THE UNIVERSITIES AND THE LEGAL INSTITUTIONS

**Educational Institutions:** Bob Jones University, Oral Roberts University, Ave Maria Law School, Christ College, Liberty University (Budget: $395.8 million), New Saint Andrews College, Patrick Henry College, Regent University ($102.7 million), University of Bridgeport.

**The Leadership Institute:** A 501(c)(3) tax-exempt organization like others, it trains, and grooms conservatives to influence public policy through activism, and teaches what it calls "political technology." It was founded in 1979 by conservative activist Morton C. Blackwell to "identify, train, recruit and place conservatives in politics, government, and media." Notable alumni include Grover Norquist, Karl Rove, Senator Mitch McConnell, Congressman Mike Pence, and seven new members of the 112th Congress.

There are several others: American Center for Law and Justice ($12.), Americans United for Life, Foundation for Moral Law, Home School Legal Defense Association, and Liberty Counsel.

**The Federalist Society:**  See, Chapter Seven

## WHY PEOPLE VOTE AGAINST THEIR ECONOMIC INTEREST?

The Party has no agenda for education, jobs, healthcare, economic growth etc. And yet millions take the bait and vote for it. All the Party does is to stir up or find a few hot-button social issues such as abortion, gay rights, and so on that whip up public emotions. Beating the drum that the "liberals" are morally decadent appeals to some. Others find the sound of lower taxes and smaller government convincing—even though it is the rich, the 1%, who benefit the most. As for smaller government, no Republican president has cut the size of government or reduced spending, including Reagan, and GW Bush. It is sheer propaganda. For the Party, Darwinism is fine in politics but not in evolution.

# VI

## THE ANTI-AMERICAN SECRET SOCIETY:

## THE COMMAND AND CONTROL CENTER

*"Does the Brotherhood exist?"*

*"That Winston, you will never know... As long as you live, it will be a riddle in your mind."* — George Orwell, *1984*

◎

Since 1981, a club of Religious Right leaders has been meeting in secrecy three times a year at undisclosed locations to strategize about how to: dismantle the democratic safety net, defeat democrats in election, keep taxes low for the rich, and steer the country toward the Right. The leaders are from all walks of life--the wealthy, large corporations, mega-churches, military, think tanks, universities, Congress, federal and state governments, media, lobbying firms, women's group. The meetings are held behind closed doors and attendees rarely speak publicly about them. The secrecy allows the members—from big oil, large banks, health insurance, big corporations, investment banks, hedge funds, venture capital firms, large law firms, and big public accounting firms--to stay out of the public eye. It allows them to be doubled-tongued and double-faced. It is perhaps no exaggeration to say that the Society has made hypocrisy a virtue in politics, big business, and religion.

What is this club? It is the Council for National Policy (CNP)—a tax-exempt 'educational organization.' The public helps finance its secret meetings and its machinations to bring down democracy. It connects the rich with the activists, bankrolls fake grassroots movement like the Tea Party, or derails Democrat's candidates in elections by launching organizations like the *"Swift Boat Veterans for Truth"* that took down John Kerry.

Its origin can be traced back to 1979 when Ed McAteer, a retired sales executive, founded the *Religious Roundtable* to back the Reagan candidacy. Soon after Reagan's victory, the CNP was founded in 1981 as the Religious Right's policy center. Start-up funding was provided by Joseph Coors, a member of Reagan's 'Kitchen Cabinet', Hunt brothers, and others. Boosted by Reagan's support, it had gathered about 400 members by 1984.

Every member is a principal but united in anti-democratic policies. Most members have their independent foundations and activist organizations. A few of the notable industrialists include; Richard Scaife; Bob J. Perry, a Texas businessman, who gave $4.5 million to *Swift Boat Veterans for Truth* in the smear campaign in 2004 that derailed John Kerry; J. Peter Grace a shipping magnate; Howard Ahmanson, a wealthy California savings-and-loan heir; Du Pont family; Elsa Prince Broekhuizen, a wealthy Michigan financier; Stuart W. Epperson, chairman of Salem Radio; Edward G. Atsinger III, President, Salem Communications; Rich DeVos, cofounder of Amway Corp; T. Cullen Davis (tried twice for murdering his daughter and wife's boyfriend); and Richard Shoff, owner of Lincoln Log Homes, and a former leader of the Ku Klux Klan.

Almost all Religious Right leaders are CNP members: Carl Rove, Ralph Reed, Grover Norquist. Tom Delay, Trent Lott, Edwin Meese, and John Ashcroft. From military, members have included, Gen. Patton, Gen. John Singlaub, Oliver North, among others. The names of the members are guarded, but a partial list can be seen on the site: [http://seekgod.ca/cnpbase.html]

A prospective member has to go through a rigorous process—a common feature of secretive organizations. A CNP member submits bio-data with the Nomination Form. The information is run through a well-guarded database. If seconded, membership is contingent on a unanimous vote by the Executive Committee, which seems to be composed of thirteen or fourteen members, including the Officers. Only then is the nominee anointed.

**Membership Rules**: ...special guests may attend only with advance unanimous approval of the Executive Committee. Council meetings are closed to the media and the general public to "allow open, uninhibited remarks" from the speakers. The media should not know when or where we meet or who takes part in our programs, before or after a meeting. Speakers' remarks at Council meetings are off the record and not for circulation later except with special permission. Members and guests are requested to keep in their personal possession their registration packets and other materials distributed at the meeting. Our membership list is strictly confidential and should not be shared outside the Council.

In-depth biographies of founders and some members reveal that many are or have been directly affiliated with such organizations as: the *John Birch Society, the Knights of Malta, Western Goals Foundation*, the *Council on Foreign Relations,* the *Unification Church of Sun Myung Moon*, the *Church of Scientology*, *Freemasonry, the CIA, Nazis,* the *Ku Klux Klan, World Anti-Communist League (WACL)* , and other racist or cult organizations. WACL was very active in the support of the *Committee for a Free Afghanistan* (CFA) which was founded in 1981 after Reagan's election and had its office space at the Heritage Foundation. The *John Birch Society* upholds the "original intent" theory for interpreting the Constitution, which it identifies with Christian principles. Eventually, it aims to dismantle the Federal Reserve System. After WW II, the *Society* helped thousands of Nazi and SS members escape justice and helped them to continue their fascist methods against communism. Another anti-communist group, *Knights of Malta's* members were founding CNP members such as Peter Grace, some from the Coors family, William Casey, James Buckley, Lee Iacocca, William Buckley, and Alexander Haig.

*CNP Action, Inc.*, an affiliate—incorporated in 1993 (right after Clinton's election)—is a (501)(c)(4) tax-exempt organization but contributions to it are not deductible. It's the lobbying arm of CNP. Its newsletter, *Capitol Hill Report*, keeps members informed of needed action and political victories. Every *CNP Action, Inc.* report ends with action items and often names specific senators and representatives to contact; it often asks that the information be passed on to interested think tanks or other groups; and sometimes asks for names of foundations, companies, or major sponsors who might help financially with an intended action.

*CNP Action*, Inc. also sponsors standing committee workshops at CNP conferences which provide a vehicle for members to work together to influence important public policy decisions. The committees' field of interest: Family, Law and Justice, Economics, Defense and Foreign Policy, Institutional Reform, and Environment.

### Should A Secretive Organization Claim Tax-Exempt Status?

When its exemption was revoked in 1992, it promised to distribute an educational journal. So the exemption was reinstalled by the IRS. CNP has never produced that journal. See [http://www.alternet.org/story/21372? page=1]

## WHAT GOES ON BEHIND THE CURTAIN?

In May 2002, ABC News ran a piece on its web site called, "Inside the Council for National Policy: Meet the Most Powerful

Conservative Group You've Never Heard Of," which quoted some high-level Bush Administration officials as speakers at a meeting at a "ritzy hotel" in Tysons Corner, Va. The article did not question the propriety or the legality of the actions of high U.S officials such as Supreme Court Justice (Clarence Thomas), White House counsel (Alberto Gonzales) and other office holders in meeting the members of a secretive organization and give secret speeches. *The New York Times in 2004* revealed—after the fact—that Vice President Dick Cheney and Secretary of Defense Donald Rumsfeld had attended a meeting "not long after the Iraq invasion." Rush Limbaugh has been a speaker at CNP meetings. On the other hand, CNP members have full access to conservative media such as Fox and Salem to disseminate their propaganda at a time of their choosing.

In May 2002, (the conservative press filled in some details) a CNP meeting took place, and Dr. Alexandr Nemets, a writer for the ultraconservative *NewsMax,* participated on a CNP panel about the war on terrorism. Dr. Nemets reported that among the 500 "prominent" attendees, several high-ranking Bush administration officials made speeches, and there was a complete uniformity of judgment that Saddam needed to be deposed with military force— ten months before the U.S. invaded Iraq during which period the Bush officials went on pretending they were trying diplomacy. Nemets further reported that the attendees had ruled out military action against other members of the axis of evil—Iran and North Korea. The Bush administration did not disclose the position it took with CNP. Why? Did it promise the Iraq war?

## WHAT DOES THE CNP DO?

Occasionally, it leaks out some information of its activities to take credit, or once in a while, some attendee talks about it. Some events remain surrounded in mystery that baffle the public.

Incidents like Clinton impeachment, or Swift Boat. The inference that CNP or one of its members had a hand in it can perhaps be drawn by a four-pronged test: 1. did it improve a Republican candidate's chances of victory, 2. did it weaken the Democratic party, 3. did it take great resources and contacts to pull it off, and, 4. Is there any other organization in the country that could have coordinated it and pulled it off in a timely fashion. Those are the footprints of CNP.

CNP itself has taken credit for a number of conservative victories in Congress: the defeat of President Clinton's health plan; Whitewater hearings; Clinton impeachment; defeat of Clinton's attempt to allow gays to serve openly in the military; sidetracking the Freedom of Choice Act; preventing the passage of the Fairness Doctrine in broadcasting; stopping the Equal Employment Opportunity Commission (EEOC) from prohibiting religious harassment in the workplace; blocking the Lobby Reform Bill; and derailing Obama healthcare's public option plan.

## Some Reported Activities

1.     CNP was instrumental in government shutdown in 1995.  See

[http://www.publiceye.org/ifas/fw/9601/cnp.html]

2.     *NY Times.com* reported on August 28, 2004 in an article "The Club of the Most Powerful Gathers in Strictest Privacy" (by David Kirkpatrick) that Bush addressed CNP in fall, 1999. The news of his speech leaked out, and Democrats demanded that the tape be released. Bush refused, and the tape has still not been made public. What was so secret? Did he promise to attack Iraq if elected? Did he promise the deep tax cuts he gave? Did he talk about "defunding" the Democrats' programs? It is known, however, that Bill Kristol, a

leading "neoconservative," a leading proponent of the Iraq War, had urged elimination of Saddam Hussein as early as 1998.

3.      In 2004, before the Republican convention, the CNP quietly convened in New York—this time almost in plain sight—at the Plaza Hotel, for what a participant called "a pep rally" to re-elect President Bush.

4.      An example of the group's far-reaching influence on the conservative is the May 9, 2006, meeting where speakers included NRA President Sandra Froman, Sen. Rick Santorum (R-Pa.), DHS Secretary Michael Chertoff, Heritage Foundation president Edwin Fuelner Jr., Phyllis Schlafly, Grover Norquist, U.S. Ambassador John Bolton, Oliver North and Robert Bork.

5.      The CNP made clear of its opposition to Rudy Giulani in 2008.

6.      Soon after the Iraq invasion, Vice President Dick Cheney and Defense Secretary Donald H. Rumsfeld attended a CNP meeting to brief it.

7.      McCain appeared before the Council in 2008 and told them what they wanted to hear: federal spending (too high), taxes (bad), dependence on foreign oil (bad), the Mexican border too porous, Iraq (a success) and, most importantly, about the judges: *I am proud to have played a role in the appointment of two of the finest judges I think that may have ever been appointed to the United States Supreme Court in Justices Alito and Roberts. I commit to you, as I have for many years, I will appoint, nominate Judges to the United States Supreme Court who strictly interpret the Constitution of the United States and do not legislate from the bench.* And, he added, "*I want to look you in the eye and tell you—I won't let you down.*"

**And One Unreported Activity: The 1980 Reagan Election and the Hostage Release**

Although CNP was founded in 1981, most of its members had been pulled together in the McAteer's *Religious Roundtable* for the express purpose of helping Reagan win the presidency.

One of the most important issues in 1980 campaign was the release of 52 Americans held hostage in Iran since November 4, 1979. On the day of Reagan's inauguration—in fact, twenty minutes after his inaugural address ended—Iran announced the release of the hostages. The timing was suspicious. Did someone in Reagan's presidential campaign conspire with Iran to delay the release until after the election?

There are documents that show that the Reagan Administration rewarded Iran by supplying weapons to it via Israel as early as March 1981. The issue raised enough controversy for the US Congress to investigate the matter. The Senate 1992 report concluded that the allegations lacked 'supporting documentation' of an 'agreement' between the Reagan campaign and Iran to delay the release of the hostages—as if such matters are documented.

But what is the evidence that a secret deal may have existed? William Casey, a *Knights of Malta* member, was the campaign manager of Reagan in 1980 (Reagan appointed him the Director of CIA from 1981 to 1987, he also oversaw covert assistance to the Mujahedeen resistance in Afghanistan later, with a budget of over $1 billion). He had international connections. He had every motive, and he had the resources.

What about direct evidence? Former Iranian President Abolhassan Bani-Sadr, Gary Sick, former Naval intelligence officer and National Security Council member, and former Reagan campaign and White House staffer, Barbara Honegger— all testified that it was William Casey, the Reagan Campaign head, who met with Iran's agents and that several meetings were held beginning with March 1980. The deal was struck between October 15–20, 1980 during meetings held in Paris between emissaries of the Reagan/Bush campaign—William Casey as the "key participant,"—and "high-level Iranian and Israeli representatives." As a result, on October 21, Iran, for inexplicable reasons, abruptly shifted its position in secret negotiations with the Carter administration and disclaimed any "further interest in receiving military equipment." The deal was that the hostages should not be released until after Reagan became president. In return, Reagan would arrange to give them arms.

Published documents show that US arms were shipped, via Israel, in March, 1981; about 2 months after Reagan became president. Banker Ernest Backes from Clearstream (Luxembourg) claimed he was in charge of the transfer of $7 million from Chase Manhattan Bank and Citibank, January 16, 1980, to pay for the liberation of the hostages. He gave copies of the files to the National French Assembly.

Equally important is the testimony of former Iranian President Abolhassan Bani-Sadr, elected President of Iran after the 1979 Iranian Revolution. He had no axe to grind in this case. In a December 17, 1992 letter he wrote to the U.S. Congress that he had first learned of the Republican "secret deal" in July 1980 after Reza Passendideh, a nephew of Khomeini, attended a meeting with Cyrus Hashemi and Republican lawyer Stanley Pottinger in Madrid on July 2, 1980. Though Passendideh was supposed to return with a proposal from Carter administration, Bani-Sadr said, Passendideh proffered instead a plan "from the Reagan camp." "Passendideh told me that if I do not accept this proposal, they [the Republicans] would make the same offer to my [radical Iranian] rivals. He further said that they [the Republicans] have enormous influence in the CIA ... Lastly, he told me my refusal of their offer would result in my elimination."

Robert Parry, an American investigative journalist, did his own sleuthing, and concluded that the House and Senate investigation committees were Kangaroo courts. According to Gary Sick's analysis of events, Oliver North was the administration's scapegoat who assumed responsibility in order to conceal the "treason" of Reagan and Bush. A PBS *Frontline* documentary in 1990 brought a sound bite of a major detail to the surface. While playing golf with George H.W. Bush in Palm Springs, Ronald Reagan told reporters he had "tried some things the other way", i.e. to free the hostages. When pressed further he added that the details remained "classified." This remark was widely publicized and linked to Reagan's 1980 undisclosed plan to free the hostages. Based on the above, the public can draw its own conclusion.

For a full report, see:
[http://www.consortiumnews.com/archive/xfile6.html]

## A FEW OTHER ACTIVITIES

### The Iran-Contra War and the Mujahedeen in 1980s

These operations were carried out with the CNP assistance. Major General Singlaub's "private" contra-supply activities were coordinated with the Reagan White House and the National Security Council (NSC). Singlaub identified former NSC aide Oliver North as his liaison to the White House. In 1984, Congress cut off CIA funds for the Contras. Secretly, Singlaub worked with North in an effort to raise millions from foreign governments. In February 1985, former Justice Department attorney John Loftus sent Congress a report detailing his suspicions that William Casey and

General Singlaub (CNP members), were using WACL and had resurrected an old private conduit system for laundering money to "freedom fighters." It was also reported that the Virginia-based Christian Broadcasting Network (CBN) of Rev. Pat Robertson (also a CNP member) was distributing aid to the contras and other Central America projects in coordination with the "Air Commandos, Refugee Relief International, World Medical Relief, Friends of the Americas, Knights of Malta and other groups."

Singlaub engaged the services of J. Peter Grace and *AmeriCares* to supply arms. He was indicted in 1986 and 1988 over activities in support of Contras for selling American weapons to Iran and skimming the proceeds to fund the President's secret wars..." Singlaub's operation was a cover for North's illegal government-sponsored supply network.

Singlaub was indicted in 1986 and 1988 over his contra activities. In an Oct 1986 interview on the CBS Television "60 Minutes," Singlaub was asked by Mike Wallace, "Let me put a thesis to you, General Singlaub. Private citizen Jack Singlaub has become Ronald Reagan's secret weapon to sidestep a Congress that will not permit him to act in the areas where he believes that our security interests are at stake. True?" Singlaub's response: "True."

The Contra activities were a core enterprise of the CNP. The Free Congress Foundation actively supported the Contras; the Heritage Foundation covertly helped Contra funding scheme. In 1985, *Heritage* "donated" $100,000 to the *Institute for North-South Issues*, a conduit to the Contras, connected to Oliver North. According to reputable international monitoring groups, the Contras, in an effort to sabotage the Nicaraguan people's support of their government, conducted a campaign of terror, murder and torture of thousands of peasants, slaughtering of livestock, and destroying villages.

Sara Diamond in *Spiritual Warfare: The Politics of the Christian Right (1990)*, said, *"The 'Contra-gate' scandal exposed that the private-aid network was not private at all, but merely a sophisticated effort to disguise the Reagan administration's deceptive dealings with foreign governments and wealthy private donors eager to finance murder and mayhem in Central America."*

By the time the sales to Iran were discovered, more than 1,500 missiles had been shipped. Three hostages held in Lebanon had been released, only to be replaced with three more, in what Secretary of State George Shultz called *"a hostage bazaar."* Reagan was investigated for illegal activities. Tower Commission concluded that as president, Reagan's disengagement from the management of his White House had created conditions which made possible the diversion of funds to the Contras. Although laws had been violated and an impeachable offense had been committed, Reagan's age and his image as a confused (incompetent?) man helped him dodge the charge. But any record of him as President will find it hard not to take this into account.

## The Clinton Impeachment

Soon after Clinton took office, a vast far-right network sprang into action to attack and discredit him. Richard Mellon Scaife, a major and consistent donor to the Religious Right, financed the *Arkansas Project* with $2.4 million and funded investigative reporting at several conservative media outlets. A *Salon* investigative report details how the Rev. Jerry Falwell and a California political organization helped finance and orchestrate an extensive anti-Clinton propaganda campaign. *Citizens for Honest Government*, a Republican activist outfit, produced an "impeachment organizers kit." The kit revealed when and where the impeachment effort was conceived —at a Montreal meeting of the CNP in June, 1997. All but five Republicans in the House voted for impeachment.

## The Tea Party

The election of any democratic President is an apocalyptic event for CNP. It goes into high gear to disrupt the Democrat's presidency by whipping up hatred and going after the midterm elections to take away the President's majority. The *Willie Horton* ad with racist undertones (that sunk Michael Dukakis in 1988 against GHW Bush); *Swift Boat* movement in 2004 election that sunk John Kerry are just a few other examples. To ensure the defeat of John Kerry as a presidential candidate in 2004, *FreedomWorks* attempted to get Ralph Nader put on the ballot in Oregon, prompting a complaint to the FEC of illegal collusion with the GOP.

Both Clinton (in 1994) and Barrack Obama (in 2010) lost their majority in the House just two years into the Office. Religious Right groups began orchestrating attacks on Obama even before he was sworn in—the *Birther* Movement was started.

The first nationwide Tea parties in February of 2009 were co-sponsored by Grover Norquist of Americans for Tax Reform, who is a charter member of the CNP. The *American Spectator*, a conservative monthly magazine that gained notoriety for articles on Clinton's sex-life, was the other sponsor. Its editor organized the rally near the White House, according to promotional materials and participants. The *Spectator* was originally funded by Richard Mellon Scaife. Former House Republican Leader Dick Armey's FreedomWorks and Americans for Prosperity (AFP), funded by the Koch family, worked behind the scene to build the *Tea Party.* In 2008, Dick Armey received $550,000 as planning for the Tea Party began. FreedomWorks assists conservative campaigns, trains volunteers and encourages them to mobilize, interacting with both fellow citizens and their political representatives. The plan for activists was to bring on board the angry Americans and infuse them with libertarian ideology.

The Libertarian party platform called for the abolition of the F.B.I. and the C.I.A., the SEC, the Department of Energy, and end Social Security, minimum-wage laws, gun control, and all personal and corporate income taxes; it proposed the legalization of prostitution, recreational drugs, and suicide. But William F. Buckley, Jr. a conservative, and himself a supporter of the laissez-faire capitalism, had called the Koch brothers ideology Anarcho-Totalitarianism.

In 2008, FreedomWorks was behind the creation of a plastic grassroots web site called Angryrenter.com which rallied opposition to "the Obama Housing Bailout." *Wall Street Journal* investigated and reported on May 16, 2008: *though it purports to be a spontaneous uprising, AngryRenter.com is actually a product of an inside-the-Beltway conservative advocacy organization led by Dick Armey, the former House majority leader, and publishing magnate Steve Forbes, a fellow Republican.*

In the weeks before the first Tax Day protests, in April, 2009, Americans for Prosperity (AFP) hosted a Web site offering supporters "Tea Party Talking Points." Peggy Venable, State Director for AFP, explained that the role of AFP was to "educate" Tea Party activists on policy details, and to give them "next-step training" after their rallies so their political energy could be channeled "more effectively." And she noted that *"AFP had provided Tea Party activists with lists of elected officials to target."* The Tea Party Movement gained national attention in the summer of 2009 when organized protests occurred at Congressional "town hall" meetings that discussed healthcare reform.

The Koch brothers funded the Tea Party; Rupert Murdoch's Fox News was part of the bus tour promotion. Karl Frisch of Media Matters wrote that Fox News "frequently aired segments imploring its audience to get involved with tea-party protests across the country." Fox News also provided organizing information for the events on air and online and gave free TV time to launch the movement by stoking fears that President Obama was a socialist. David Axelrod, Obama's senior adviser, said, *"What they don't say is that, in part, this is a grassroots citizens' movement brought to you by a bunch of oil billionaires."*

Less than a year away from the 2012 presidential election, right-wing extremists are waging war through these AstroTurf movements—nationally and in the states—to break democrats' voter-funding base of labor, government employees, and teacher unions. Those who are taken in by the movement to wage war on the middle class will finally see how they have been used. Then it might be too late.

Ensuring Liberty Corp, a support group, was set up as a social welfare 501(c)(4) organization to raise funds for the Tea Party movement. Such organizations are not required to disclose their donors and can raise funds without limits from the wealthy donors. In 2010, a bill requiring identification of donors was passed in House but was defeated in the Senate.

Bob Cesca wrote in Huffington Post on March 3, 2010: *The Tea party is an extension of talk radio. It's an extension of Fox News Channel. It's an extension of the southern faction of the Republican Party— the faction that gave us the Southern Strategy, the Willie Horton ad, the White Hands ad and the racially divisive politics of Lee Atwater and Karl Rove. When you throw out all of the nonsense and contradictions, there's nothing left except race... A white candidate would never be accused of being a secret Muslim... Can any conscientious Christian really believe that someone who loves*

*Jesus Christ will knowingly join with and have the same beliefs or goals as a Nazi, or follow Sun Myung Moon—who believes himself to be Messiah.*

In the last four decades, in its unethical pursuit of power, the Republicans have paid little heed to the laws of the nation and the basics of democracy. The Party's arrogance is apparent on many fronts. To a waitress who asked him (April 4, 2006) to put out his cigar because smoking in a restaurant in Washington was against Federal law, Tom Delay replied*: I am the Federal Government.*

# VII

## YOUR HONOR! ENJOY THE DONKEY BURGER!

## THE SUPREME COURT

*Three Philadelphia lawyers are a match for the Devil.*–Mencken: A New England Proverb (*And Five?*)

◎

To harness lawyers and judges for the rightwing cause, Joseph Coors had formed "The Rocky Mountain Legal Foundation" in 1976 to circumvent the "green" laws passed in early 1970s. Once Reagan was in the White House in 1980, however, Edwin Meese III, a conservative, and a close Reagan friend, also called the Lenin of the movement (Salon.com), embarked on an ambitious plan to solidify the Religious Right for the long haul. Coors, now a member of Reagan's "Kitchen Cabinet," and Meese, in addition to creating several other organizations, embarked on a program to change the "culture" of the Supreme Court.

The Federalist Society was set up in 1982 with several friends and colleagues—including Robert Bork, and future Supreme Court Justice William Rehnquist, William Kristol, David M. McIntosh, Steven Calabresi, Antonin Scalia, and Samuel Alito. The Society was generously funded by Richard Mellon Scaife and Koch brothers, among others. Kenneth W. Starr, whose report led to Clinton's impeachment, is a prominent member, as is Theodore B. Olson, who successfully argued *Bush v. Gore*, the case that stopped the Florida recount in 2000 and handed victory to GW Bush. The *Society* has received over $12 million in grants since 1985. Its lawyers division has over 30,000 practicing attorneys, more than

5,000 law students at 145 law schools, and a new Faculty Division with unpublished membership numbers.

The *Society* quickly became a national networking organization that nurtured young conservatives and became a crucial channel to Supreme Court clerkships and prestigious jobs in the Reagan administration. Influence pedaling and allegations of corruption and bribery, the cover-up of sale of arms in the Iran-Contra affair, led Meese to resign. From the White House, he walked over to the *Heritage Foundation*, which had greatly benefitted from his position in the White House. The *Federalist Society* has transformed the US legal system by promoting far-right positions and influencing judges, top government officials, and decision-makers.

## THE SOCIETY'S AGENDA

Federalist Society is an important part of the vast network of rightwing institutions that the GOP has built over three decades. The idea behind Federal Society was to make top judges accessible to the rich, to indoctrinate lawyers and law students in the ideology of Dominionism that includes "free markets." Like other Religious Right organizations, the Society is hostile to civil rights, reproductive choice, healthcare, environmental protections, worker safety laws, business regulation, and separation between church and state. It stands for states' rights against the federal government.

### A Gimmick Created For Subverting the Constitution

The Constitution has been interpreted for over two centuries by judges. Their interpretation advanced democracy in America, and the nation prospered. Can a gimmick subvert the Constitution?

Yes, it can, says the Religious Right—by interpreting the Constitution through the prism of ideology. It is called interpreting the Constitution according to the "original intent" of the Framers of the Constitution.

Speaking at Tulane University in October 1986, Meese made a distinction between the Constitution and the Constitutional law. Constitutional law, he said, is that body of law which has resulted from the Supreme Court's decisions. He suggested that to be understood, the Constitution needs to be read without the interpretations made by the judges. To him the meaning of Constitution was fixed in time.

Harry Jaffa (See, Chapter 4), a political philosophy teacher, and a student of Strauss (who taught at Chicago and resurrected Machiavelli, and influenced the "neo-conservatives") did not accept the view that Constitution was secular or based on social contract. Jaffa believed that the *Declaration of Independence* was the premier document that superseded the Constitution: "The Declaration...is the charter of the nation. It is what you might call the articles of incorporation, whereas the Constitution is the bylaws. The Constitution is the means by which to carry out the great purposes (life, liberty, and pursuit of happiness) that are articulated in the Declaration." So the Constitution has to be seen in light of the *Declaration* to determine the 'original intent' of the Framers. The doctrine enables judges to apply the rightwing ideology under the cover of "original intent."

The question is whether after 220 years it possible to ascertain the "original intent"? Often, there are contradictions between what happened and the Framers' intent. For example, in the case of Senate, the Framers wanted proportional representation but were blackmailed/bribed/coerced to accept an equal number of Senators from each state. That's why Wyoming has two senators, and California has two.  If challenged, would the Supreme Court go back to the "original intent"?

## THE FRAMERS' 'INTENT'

Significantly, the Framers discouraged any attempt to look for "original intent" in future.  By beginning the document with "We the People" the Framers did not wish to claim a greater authority for themselves. In Madison's words, they were "mere scriveners." Madison went on to stress that the meaning of the Constitution was determined by an interpretive process that would continue long after the Philadelphia and State Conventions had closed their doors. As President, Madison signed the Second Bank Bill into law even though as a representative in the First Congress he had opposed the bill because he believed Congress had no constitutional right to establish a national bank. But he came to recognize that "Congress, the President, the Supreme Court, and most importantly, the American people had for two decades accepted the existence and made use of the services of the First Bank." Madison viewed this widespread acceptance, he said as "*a construction put on the Constitution by the nation, which, having made it had the supreme right to declare its meaning.*"

Thus, the Constitution's meaning is to be found in the history of interpretations and the constitutional law rather than what the Framers originally had in mind. In other words, the Framers' first words—the text—were suggestive but not final. There is no last word.  The interpretation of Constitution is an ongoing process. It has to be in the interest of an orderly evolution of democracy. Most experts believe that the Constitution was created to establish a strong central government that can govern the Union effectively, and that the Framers intended the Constitution to accommodate each new generation and new circumstance. All of this is being targeted by the "original intent."

## THE INTENT BEHIND THE "ORIGINAL INTENT"

Stripped of all legalese and rationalizations, Federalist Society is an arm of the Religious Right. It was created for the rightwing judges to help them apply the ideology of Dominionism to Constitution. Dominionism rejects separation between Church and State, and embraces "free markets." Religious Right leaders play a dominant role in the *Society*. Former President of the *Christian Coalition*, Donald Hodel is a board member. Leonard A. Leo, the head of Catholic outreach for the Republican Party, took leave of absence to help Judge Roberts win confirmation in the Senate.

In *Closed Chambers: The Rise, Fall, and Future of the Modern Supreme Court (2005)*, Lazarus, former law clerk to Justice Harry Blackmun, reveals how Federalist Society clerks formed a self-described "cabal against the libs" to push justices in rightward direction. Twenty-four of Bush's top cabinet hardcore conservative members, and most of his court nominations, came from the Federalist Society. Among them: John Ashcroft, Attorney General; Spencer Abraham, Secretary of Energy; Gail Norton, Secretary of the Interior; and Theodore Olson, Solicitor General, and John Yoo, Department of Justice. The *Society* accused the American Bar Association (ABA) of liberal bias in recommendations. So GW Bush terminated the ABA's long tradition of rating judicial nominees' qualifications.

To deflect Democrats' concerns, the Court nominees have repeatedly claimed to know nothing or little about the group's beliefs and tried to distance themselves from it. After Bush tapped John G. Roberts Jr. for the Supreme Court, Roberts was questioned about his membership in the *Society*. He feigned lapse of memory. Dana Perino, a Bush administration spokeswoman, told the paper that Roberts "has no recollection of being a member of the Federalist Society, or its steering committee." *The Washington Post* got hold of the 1997-1998 Federalist Society's Lawyers' Division Leadership Directory that showed Roberts as one of the leaders of the group. The future Chief Justice was lying before the Senate. Why? Because he knew that the *Society* is an anti-Democratic organization engaged in advancing the GOP agenda. Senator Orrin G. Hatch, a Utah Republican on the Judiciary Committee, blurted out the truth. "I am on the board of advisers of the Federalist Society, and I am darn proud of it," he said. He called the *Society* a group of lawyers "who are just sick and tired of the leftward leanings of our government."

Guido Calabresi, one of the founders of the *Society*, a federal appeals court judge, says, "The Federalist Society was, when it got started, a wonderful idea." But he worries that its career-advancement role invites distrust and promotes conformity. "*It becomes something of a secret society*," he said.

## SEPARATION BETWEEN CHURCH AND STATE

Let us first see what the Constitution says.

First Amendment: Congress shall make no law respecting an establishment of religion, or prohibiting the free exercise thereof.

Article VI, Para 3, last sentence: No religious test shall ever be required as a Qualification to any Office or public Trust under the United States.

In his 1802 letter to the Danbury Baptist Association, late President Jefferson said: ...Legislature should make no law respecting an establishment of religion, or prohibiting the free exercise thereof, thus building a wall of separation between church and state.

In *Lemon v Kurtzman* (403 US 602 [1971], the Court spoke of the three main evils against which the Establishment Clause was intended to afford protection: "sponsorship, financial support, and active involvement of the sovereign in religious activity."

## The Position of the Religious Right

The Bible has supremacy over the U.S. Constitution. Period. Several rightwing organizations like The Alliance Defense Fund, and the Rutherford Institute have sprung up to defend the teaching of Creationism in schools in place of Darwin's evolution. Christian law schools, including those set up by Pat Robertson and Jerry Falwell (like Liberty University School of Law) have been training young lawyers to think in terms of biblical worldview.

## Court Stripping

The Religious Right leaders take the view that the courts can be stripped of their powers to review cases of a religious nature. Katherine Yurica has transcripts of Pat Robertson's television show, the *700 Club*, from 1985 where he explained his strategy to strip the federal judiciary of its constitutional powers: Robertson denied that the Constitution provides a system of checks and balances between three separate and equal branches of government. Instead, he saw the judiciary as a department of the legislative branch since Congress has complete authority to establish the lower federal courts and to establish "the appellate jurisdiction of the Supreme Court." Hence the court system is subordinate to the legislature. Robertson wants Congress to tell the courts, 'There's a whole class of cases you can't hear," and nobody can do "anything about it!" The Right has tried to: inject religion into public schools through teacher-led school prayer in the classroom; obtain taxpayer funding for religious schools and other church ministries and openly attacked the Constitution.

Gary North, a Christian Reconstruction writer, and founder of the Institute for Christian Economics, wrote in *Christianity and Civilization*, Spring, 1982*: "So let us be blunt about it: we must use the doctrine of religious liberty to gain independence for Christian schools until we train up a generation of people who know that there is no religious neutrality, no neutral law, no neutral education, and no neutral civil government. Then they will get busy in constructing a Bible-based social, political and religious order which finally denies the religious liberty to the enemies of God."*

## Court Stripping by the US Congress

The *Constitution Restoration Act of 2004* was the ultimate court-stripping measure. It included the acknowledgment of God as the sovereign source of law, and threatened those judges with "impeachment" and "conviction" who uphold church-state separation. Though it failed, the situation can change any time when all the three branches of government are under GOP control. In the 2012 crop of Republican presidential primaries, Michel Bachmann, Rick Santorum and Newt Gingrich have supported this position.

## The Supreme Court's Position

While other rightwing justices have not spoken, Justice Scalia has. In an article published in *First Things,* a journal of religion and public life, in May, 2002, Scalia quotes St. Paul: "...Government...derives its moral authority from God. It is the minister of God with powers to "avenge" to "execute wrath" including even wrath by the sword (a reference to the death penalty)."

In another speech on January 12, 2003, at a Religious Freedom Day event, Justice Scalia said that the church state separation principle was not imbedded in the Constitution. He asserted that Founding Fathers never meant to "exclude God from the public forums and from political life." In his article *God's Justice and Ours*, Scalia explained how he would determine whether the death penalty was constitutional or not. His reasoning: since the death penalty was "clearly permitted when the Eighth Amendment [which prohibits 'cruel and unusual punishments'] was adopted," and at that time the death penalty was applied for all felonies— including, for example, the felony of horse-thieving, "so it is clearly permitted today." That is "original intent" in action. A Dominionist Republican controlled Congress is likely to extend the death penalty to all persons committing witchcraft, adultery, homosexuality, heresy, etc. And it would all be constitutional according to the rightwing justices when they have the majority.

## Faith-based Initiatives and Discrimination in Hiring

The Civil Rights Act, signed into law in 1964, banned discrimination in employment on the basis of race, gender, or religion. The Religious Right disregards the Civil Rights Act. To enact his program of Faith Based Initiative—a device to pump money into the churches, GW Bush circumvented the Civil Rights Act, as reported in *Church and State*, September, 2003. By a 217-216 vote on July 25, the House passed a bill (H.R.2210) that permitted religious groups operating *Head Start Centers* to discriminate in hiring.

## 'Free Markets' Theory And the Supreme Court

The dismantling of the "Safety Net" and instituting the "free market" economy is an important part of the Federalist Society's agenda. James Robison, a televangelist convened two recent meetings of Christian Right leaders in Texas to ponder their role in

2012. Talking about the "free market" part of his agenda, he said: Those we elect must keep the free market free, healthy and under the influence of people who understand the importance of personal responsibility. He brushed aside concerns about inequality.

The second line of attack concerning the federal powers has come from the Tea Party. It is opposed to the Supreme Court decisions that enabled the federal government to enact New Deal programs like Social Security and Medicare that protect people afflicted by "personal failure" from the consequences of their actions. Earlier, President Reagan had expressed the same view. The two lines—personal responsibility, and New Deal—had been thus merged under the "free market" umbrella.

## Tactics in Securing Judicial Appointments

As mentioned in the Chapter on Constitution, the Senate has to ratify President's appointments to federal judiciary—a procedure that used to take just a few weeks. Now it is being increasingly abused by Republicans by withholding confirmations for over two years on the basis of failing to meet *their* ideological litmus test or guilt by association—perhaps in anticipation of a Republican president in 2012. At the end of September 2011, there were 115 vacancies.

California Supreme Court Justice Goodwin Liu was nominated to the federal appeals bench in February 2010 but withdrew in May 2011 because of the GOP filibuster on ground of his liberal leanings. U.S. District Judge Edward Chen's confirmation took almost two years. The right wing smear machine accused him of being a radical who recoiled at the sound of "America the Beautiful."

The movement simply continues to build up new talent in the off-years, even without Republican administrations, noted Ian Millhiser, a legal policy analyst at the *Center for American Progress*. The Democrats just haven't done that. Millhiser said, "When Bush was in office, he nominated a very successful round of hardcore movement conservatives, some of whom received resistance...but many of them didn't receive any resistance at all...the Democratic senators pretty much rolled over, because they didn't view this as an important enough issue." Furthermore, he said, "When there's a conservative president, the Federalist Society can give a list of names to that conservative president that they want to see nominated. And when there's a progressive president, then the Federalist Society can work with their allies in the Senate to make sure that the movement progressives in this (Obama) administration, really any judges—don't get confirmed. Then they hold their slots open..." According to the *Washington Post*, Ed Meese had worked behind scenes to stop the confirmation of Sonia Sotomayor.

## IS THE SUPREME COURT STILL INDEPENDENT?

Starting with Ronald Reagan, the Supreme Court has been studded with right wing justices: Scalia, Alioto, Thomas, Roberts, who are often assisted by Kennedy. While denouncing judicial activism, all these appointees were judicial activists with an agenda. They treat Second Amendment as if local militias are still necessary, to them money is "speech," and corporations are "people," America is a confederation so the states' rights must be resurrected; they treat the Commerce Clause as if America is an island—immune from global economy.

Though the *Society* takes few official positions, much of the influence, and much of the intrigue, flows from an informal social network, where members advance one another's causes and careers. Openly and behind the scenes, members have played prominent roles in the most pitched political battles in recent years, including the impeachment of President Bill Clinton and the Florida recount fracas in 2000 that led to the election of GW Bush. In the 1990's, three Federalist Society lawyers, Jerome M. Marcus, Richard W. Porter and George T. Conway, played important but covert roles in helping Paula Jones sue President Clinton for sexual harassment. They also worked behind the scenes to disclose Clinton's affair with a White House intern, Monica Lewinsky.

By politicizing judiciary, the *Society* is jeopardizing the principle of independent judiciary—a fundamental tenet of the Constitution and indispensable to the healthy functioning of democracy.

## THE CORRUPTION IN THE JUDICIARY

The *NY Times* (Jan, 2011) reported that in 2010 the votes of Thomas and Scalia swung the Court in the direction of the right-wing group *Citizens United* case that struck down federal campaign-finance reform law limiting corporate campaign contributions.

Before the decision, Thomas and Scalia also participated in a political retreat hosted by Tea Party financiers Charles and David Koch. Back in 1991 when Thomas was nominated to the Supreme Court, *Citizens United* spent $100,000 to support his nomination. The in-kind contribution presumably should have been disclosed by Thomas. At the very least, given his connections with *Citizen's United* and Koch brothers, Thomas should have recused himself from the *Citizens United* to avoid the appearance of a conflict-of-interest.

In December 2010 Scalia met in a closed-door session with Michele Bachmann's *Tea Party Caucus*, a group formed in large part to fight for the repeal of healthcare reform. In January 2011, the liberal advocacy group *Common Cause* reported that between 2003 and 2007 Thomas failed to disclose $686,589 in income earned by his wife from the *Heritage Foundation* on his Supreme Court financial disclosure forms. The matter was reported to the U.S. Judicial Conference, the agency that collects judicial disclosure forms. When caught, Thomas stated the following week that the disclosure of his wife's income had been "inadvertently omitted due to a misunderstanding (stretching over 20 years?) of the filing instructions." Thomas amended reports going back to 1989. Justice Thomas is known for his contempt for blacks for not taking personal responsibility. But what about his own personal responsibility? Is he exempt from it in his own eyes?

Though the employment and political activism of the justice's wife, Virginia "Ginni" Thomas, was no secret, Justice Thomas had failed to report her work on Capitol Hill for then-Rep. Dick Armey in the mid-1990s, for the *Heritage Foundation* from 1998-2007, and for Hillsdale College in 2008. Virginia Thomas is the founder of *Liberty Central*, a Tea Party organization now receiving unlimited corporate contributions from Koch brothers—thanks to *Citizens United* decision. Among the things she's lobbying for are the repeal of what she terms the "unconstitutional" Obama healthcare legislation.

Because of his wife's direct involvement, 74 House Democrats have sent a letter to Justice Thomas asking him to recuse himself from any case questioning the constitutionality of the legislation. "Your spouse is advertising herself as a lobbyist who has 'experience and connections' and appeals to clients who want a particular decision," the legislators wrote. "They want to overturn health-care reform."

Like other federal officials, justices are required to annually report the sources of "non-investment" income by spouses. It's the law, part of the Ethics in Government Act of 1978, and it seems clear that Justice Thomas was in violation. The Ethics Act carries both civil and criminal penalties for anyone who "knowingly and willfully falsifies" or fails to file a disclosure report. The maximum penalty is a $50,000 fine and one year in prison. So, should Justice Thomas be prosecuted?

If the answer is yes, then the question is: Can he be prosecuted – given that he holds a lifetime appointment. Can be removed from office only through impeachment? But the revelations seem to indicate that Justice Thomas is not merely guilty of multiple conflicts of interest, he may have also lied about it. And that's an impeachable offense, as Clinton found out.

Questions were also raised about the retreat. The event was organized by Charles and David Koch. A court spokeswoman said Justice Thomas had made a "brief drop-by" at the event in Palm Springs, Calif., in January 2008 and had given a talk. In his financial disclosure report for that year, however, Justice Thomas reported that the Federalist Society had reimbursed him an undisclosed amount for four days of "transportation, meals and accommodations" over the weekend of the retreat. But the retreat was organized by Kock brothers. Why did the Federalist Society reimburse him? Is the Society a cover for Koch brothers and others? And for the rich who meet in secret with the Supreme Court judges before an important case is about to come before them, entertain them, invite them to retreats, and then have the *Society* reimburse them because reimbursing them directly may look like a bribe.

Arn Pearson, vice president at the advocacy group *Common Cause*, said the two statements appeared at odds. His group sent a letter to the Supreme Court asking for "further clarification" as to whether the justice spent four days at the retreat for the entire event or was he there only briefly. "I don't think the explanation they've given is credible," Pearson said in an interview. He said that if Justice Thomas's visit was a "four-day, all-expenses paid trip in sunny Palm Springs," it should have been reported as a gift under federal law. Thomas failed to disclose, just as he had failed to disclose the financial information about his wife's employment and earnings.

House Rules Committee ranking member Louise Slaughter (D-N.Y.) and Rep. Earl Blumenauer (D-Ore.) have sent a letter to the House Judiciary Committee calling for hearings "on the pattern of potential ethical lapses" by Thomas, who failed to disclose his wife Ginny's employment status every year between 1997 and 2011. During that time, the letter states, his wife made at least $1.6 million based on public reports. In addition, reports indicate that Justice Thomas may have also failed to report gifts from wealthy supporters and inappropriately solicited donations for favored non-profit organizations. Specifically, her past employers included the Heritage Foundation, which paid her hundreds of thousands of dollars between 2003 to 2007 alone. The Heritage Foundation was a major opponent of the Affordable Care Act—a law on which the Supreme Court is expected to rule on by next summer. Slaughter and 19 other Democratic lawmakers have called for Justice Department investigation. Justice Thomas should volunteer to resign amid these serious charges. Or greed trumps self-respect?

Hours after the justices decided to hear challenge to national health care reform law, Justices Thomas and Antonin Scalia attended on November 10, 2011 a Federalist Society fundraiser sponsored in part by law firms engaged to litigate the law—a breach of ethical standards that apply to federal judges. Justice

Samuel Alito, a regular at Federalist Society gatherings, was in the audience. Guests at Scalia's table at the Federalist Society dinner included Sen. Minority Leader Mitch McConnell, who at last year's Federalist Society annual conference was actively recruiting members of the group to join him in efforts to overturn the health care law. Is this an independent Supreme Court?

# VIII

## MR. PRESIDENT! TEAR DOWN THE SAFETY NET WALL!

## THE GOP FISCAL RECORD

*"In constitutional states liberty is compensation for the heavy taxation; in despotic states the equivalent of liberty is light taxes."* – Montesquieu: The Spirit of the Laws XIII

⓪

Speaking on the Senate floor on Jul 13, 2011, Senate Minority Leader Mitch McConnell (R-KY) observed that America must rewrite the Constitution: "The time has come for a balanced budget amendment that forces Washington to balance its books...to get our fiscal house in order...*We've tried negotiations. We've tried elections. Nothing has worked* (emphasis added)."

Only if he had spoken the truth! *Just once!*

There was a time, many may have forgotten, when the Republican party stood for fiscal conservatism. Theodore Roosevelt enforced anti-trust law, and created the modern National Park Service. Eisenhower warned against the dominance of industrial-military establishment. Even Nixon established the Environmental Protection Agency. Then in the late 1960s, everything changed.

We need to clarify here the difference between budget deficit and the national debt. Budget deficit is the shortfall between government revenues and expenditures during a single year. The national debt is the accumulation of the budget deficits over the years.

## THE DEMOCRATS RECORD

Though this chapter's emphasis is on the Republican fiscal record in the last four decades, it is necessary not to overlook the Democrats' record—to see how that stacks up against the Republicans.

Carter (1977-1980) ran a deficit in each of his four years, and added $482.8 billion to the national debt. Carter dropped the number of federal employees by 14,000.

Clinton ran deficits in each of its first four years and a surplus in each of the last four years. The Clinton years paid down a net $14.2 billion of national debt and averaged a surplus of $1.78 billion during the eight years. So, at the end of 2000, the Democrats as a party had created a net surplus of $9.4 billion. The economy grew in each of the eight Clinton years at an average of 3.5%. Clinton reduced the size of federal government by 105,000 employees.

## THE REPUBLICANS RECORD

### Nixon-Ford Years (1968-76)

Since the 1944 Breton Woods Agreement, America had followed the Gold Standard. Richard Nixon, however, dumped the gold standard without ado. The U.S was now free to print and spend recklessly. Financial volatility surged. Nixon accepted Milton Friedman's theory that the "free market" was the best mechanism for setting currency exchange rates, and that "trade deficits will self-correct." So Nixon became the first Republican president to endorse deficit spending to stimulate the economy. Nixon (and

Ford) also added 213,000 federal (non-defense) employees. The Nixon and Ford administrations ran deficits in each of their eight years. The Nixon-Ford budgets averaged a yearly deficit of $87.84 billion for a total of $702.7 billion to the national debt. See [http://sideshow.me.uk/annex/JustForTheRecord.htm]

## REAGAN

**Reagan's Promise from His 1980 Election Agenda**: *Reduce tax rates on individuals and businesses. Limit government spending to a fixed and smaller percentage of the Gross National Product. Balance the budget without tax increases (at these lower levels of taxation and spending). If necessary, seek to adopt a Constitutional amendment to limit federal spending and balance the budget.*

### Reagan's Record: Taxes

Reagan lowered the taxes in his first year just as he had promised: the top marginal individual income tax rate first fell from 70% to 50% and then to 28% for top earners, and the bottom rates fell from 14% to 11%. Later, when the deficits rose, he did raise taxes several times—mostly the Social Security payroll taxes—that mostly hit the middle and lower wage earners. The capital gains tax was reduced from 28% to 20%. This mainly benefitted the opulent class.

### Reagan's Spending Record

During his term (FY1981-FY1989), Reagan ran huge budget deficits in each of his eight years. In time of peace, he expanded the U.S. military budget by a staggering 43% over the total expenditure at the height of the Vietnam war as a result of his Strategic Defense Initiative (SDI)—dubbed "Star Wars." The U.S. had to borrow both domestically and abroad to cover the huge deficits. The national debt went up from $997 billion to $2.85

trillion; he tripled the national debt. From being the world's largest international creditor, the U.S. became the world's largest debtor nation.

While always telling the public "government is the problem, not the solution," he increased the number of federal employees by 238,000. Two hundred thirty eight thousand! Instead of solving the problem, he greatly increased it. He led the transformation of the US economy from a manufacturing economy to a financial economy—the rise of the Wall Street. Large numbers of US jobs were outsourced. The number of Americans below the poverty level increased from 29.3 million in 1980 to 31.7 million in 1988, while the incomes of the top wage earners tripled or quadrupled. In the closing weeks of his presidency, Reagan told the *New York Times* that the homeless *"make it their own choice for staying out there."*

## Reagan, the Economist, On 'Supply Side'

Reagan embraced "supply side" economics, also known as Laffer curve. Its author, Laffer, is said to have explained this theory to some congressman in the 1970s on a dinner napkin. It states that if tax rates are cut, productivity and investment will increase dramatically so total tax revenues will rise and debt will be reduced. It was "trickle-down economics." Like water coming down the mountain top? Lower taxes were also advocated by the "free market" theorists like Frederic Van Hayek and Milton Friedman—but only if tax cuts were matched with cuts in spending. Their free market theory advocated fiscal conservatism and restraint.

## The Record of 'Supply Side' Economics

The Reagan tax cuts did not increase the GDP growth rate or productivity. In fact, the Reagan's tax cuts greatly increased the deficit. True, the economy grew from 1983 to 1989 due to the fact that the economy was coming out of the severe recession of 1981-1982 when the unemployment rate had climbed to over 10%, interest rates to 20%, and inflation to 18%. As energy prices plunged, interest rates came down, and normal growth resumed, the economy created 22 million jobs (for the record, Clinton increased tax rates and created 23 million jobs. And produced budget surplus). The public debt ratio to GDP increased from 26.1% in 1979 to 41.2% in 1986! In effect, Reagan funded the tax cuts for the rich with borrowed funds. He launched an era of increasing the national debt. We look down at Greece today for spending with borrowed funds. But Reagan did exactly that in the 1980s. The steep debts deeply eroded the faith of people in their government. By the mid-1990s, the federal deficit, and efforts to reduce it, had become national preoccupation.

## THE 'SUPPLY SIDE' STORY IN REPUBLICANS' OWN WORDS

The 'supply side' economics had never been shown to have worked in any country. As opponent of Reagan in the 1980 presidential primaries, George H.W. Bush called this—"voodoo economics."

Perhaps, the most honest criticism of supply side economics came from Reagan's own man—David Stockman, the wonder kid of the Reagan administration, and the director of the Office of Management and Budget. Back in 1981, Stockman was brought in to show in actual budget the trickle-down miracle Reagan had promised: that lower taxes lead to lower budgets, lower spending, and higher tax revenue. But Stockman knew that trickle-down economics was a gimmick to get votes and to give tax cuts to the rich. And Reagan knew it. Stockman was put in charge of the plan of "the greatest transfer of wealth within any society in the history of man": the shifting of the tax burden from Capital to Labor. From the rich to the working class. One evening after a few drinks, Stockman confided his feelings about an intellectually dishonest, politically corrupt federal budget process to William Greider of *The Atlantic Monthly*; the president's tax cut, he claimed, was a "Trojan horse" that promised reductions for everyone but was really designed to reduce the tax rates of the rich at the top. It came out in the magazine and all hell broke loose. He had committed the one unpardonable sin in the Republican party: he told the truth. Outraged that the Budget Director had spilled the beans, Reagan took him out "to the woods" and he had to leave.

In *How My G.O.P. Destroyed the U.S. Economy,*** David Stockman tells us that Reagan put, "...Huge debt burdens on future generations...the defense budget soared out of control ...Reagan was utterly uninterested in any detail of the defense budget...he gave them (Pentagon) a blank check, that ... ballooned spending just as we were massively reducing the revenue (by huge tax breaks to the superrich)."

**[http://www.nytimes.com/2010/08/01/opinion/01stockman.html?pagewanted=all], in a *New York Times* op-ed piece (*Four Deformations of the Apocalypse*)

The Nobel laureate economist Paul Krugman did a detailed analysis of 'supply side' economics in *Peddling Prosperity* (Norton, 1995) and reached a similar conclusion. The supply-siders (the economists from whom the rightwing strategists borrowed the phrase to make it look respectable) on whom Reagan relied, advocated a gold standard--that Nixon had scrapped-- so money growth was checked and spending kept within limits. But Reagan spending record was unprecedented in U.S history. James Tobin, an economist on Board of Governors of the Federal Reserve System, called it worthy of "ridicule" in a 1992 article in the *Harvard International Review*.

Kevin Philips, a conservative Republican strategist in the 1970s, was astonished by what he saw: an inhospitable, ungovernable Republican party with Reagan as its leader, "pocked by craters of ideological fervor, fiscal insanity, and unspeakable personal greed." Disillusioned by the party's fiscal irresponsibility and kowtowing of war establishment, oil interests, and the Religious Right, he left politics and joined the academia. He said that the Reagan tax cuts were primarily aimed at increasing the wealth and political power of the Wall Street investment banks like Goldman Sachs, Morgan Stanley, and Lehman Brothers. The multinationals pocketed their hefty tax breaks, and kept laying off American workers while creating jobs in other countries. The conversion of American manufacturing economy to financial economy--started by Reagan--finally pulled down the economy in 2008.

## REAGAN SPENDING: A PLOY TO DEFUND THE SAFETY NET?

Like all Reagan initiatives, the idea of Strategic Defense Initiative (SDI) came directly from a CNP member—Lt. General Daniel Graham, a former director of the U.S. Defense Intelligence Agency (DIA). Graham was an important figure in Rev. Moon's CAUSA, the political arm of the Moonie Unification Church. Graham, like Singlaub, and other CNP members, exerted great influence on Reagan. Lev Dobriansky, a former OSS officer in Germany in World War II, and a member of the U.S. arm of WACL in the 1970s, had the support of Graham and Singlaub. So Reagan appointed him U.S. ambassador to the Bahamas. Reagan went further: Dobriansky's daughter, Paula, was appointed to the National Security Council. And SDI was on CNP's agenda. Even the Pentagon knew it was unworkable and a piece of fiction. Reagan, an otherwise fiscal conservative, was suddenly transformed into a dreamer and recklessly kept spending on SDI despite massive budget deficits.

Lowering the taxes and running huge deficits was not in Reagan's character—till he came to White House. He had presided over an astonishing expansion of taxes in California as governor and created a budget surplus.

## Explosion of National Debt

It is no secret that Reagan came into office with the push from the Moral Majority, an enterprise of the Religious Right establishment. One of avowed goals of the Religious Right was (and has continued to this day) to "defund" the safety-net by "starving the beast." The ultimate objective was—and still is—to demolish the Democrat's voter base. To that end, military expenditure was a clever pretext-- Congress could not refuse the request, and the people would not suspect. SDI program was supported by the Heritage Foundation—a CNP members enterprise.

All Reagan's actions point in that direction. His administration was practically run by the Heritage Foundation; Joseph Coors, the beer baron, sat in Reagan's "Kitchen Cabinet." The Right's agenda became Reagan's agenda. He channeled billions of dollars and sophisticated weapons through Pakistan's intelligence agency to fund, train, arm, and equip the Mujahidin in Afghanistan to combat the Soviets (threat of communism in a country as small, and as distant from America as Afghanistan!). He failed to see  the consequences of his actions—Al Qaeda and the Taliban that resulted directly from his actions in Afghanistan and came to haunt America within years after he left.

Reagan abandoned caution in carrying out the rightwing agenda, and got involved in illegally activities—sale of arms to Iran to secretly support anti-Communist activities in Nicaragua. And when he got in trouble, he blamed his memory—on the advice of his officials—to get out of the jam. He had no agenda of his own for the people. He had no convictions of his own: a liberal Democrat in his youth, he became a liberal Republican under the influence of his employer General Electric. As Governor of California, he liberalized California's abortion laws in 1967 that led to two million abortions. Then CNP and the Heritage Foundation (Religious Right) appeared on the scene, and he became a conservative, and pro-life. His lack of political experience, lack of judgment, lack of conscience, and lack of intellect was unscrupulously manipulated by the rightwing.

He helped create rightwing organizations such as the CNP (1981), the Federalist Society (1982), the Washington Times (1982), Americans for Tax Reform (1985). He stacked the Supreme Court and federal courts with right wing judges; his deregulatory policies led to savings and loan crisis in the late 1980s when 747 out of the 3,234 savings and loan associations went bankrupt. He encouraged and strengthened a party focused on dividing the nation. He was the "great divider"--an anti-thesis of Abraham Lincoln.

This account of Reagan—that he spent outrageously to defund the safety net--is corroborated by the economist Von Hayek, a Reagan friend. The "free market" guru, Friederich von Hayek did not buy into Reaganomics. In the March 25, 1985 issue of *Profil 13*, the Austrian journal, he sat for an interview while wearing a set of cuff links Reagan had previously presented to him. *"I really believe Reagan is fundamentally a decent and honest man,"* von Hayek told his interviewer. *"His politics? When the government of the United States borrows a large part of the savings of the world, the consequence is that capital must become scarce and expensive in the whole world. That's a problem."* Hayek was disillusioned with Reagan's misunderstanding and misapplication of his theories. And in reference to Stockman, von Hayek said: *"You see, one of Reagan's advisers told me why the president has permitted that (big deficits) to happen, which makes the matter partly excusable: Reagan thinks it is impossible to persuade Congress that expenditures must be reduced unless one creates deficits so large*

115

*that absolutely everyone becomes convinced that no more money can be spent."* He went on*: it was up to Reagan to "persuade Congress of the necessity of spending reductions. Unfortunately, he has not succeeded!!!"* Those three exclamation points are in the original. In other words, Reagan led the country down the lane of economic ruin so Congress will be forced to dismantle the safety net programs!

In *Why I Am Not a Conservative,* (included as an appendix to *The Constitution of Liberty* (University of Chicago Press, (1960)), Von Hayek goes further. He disparaged conservatism for its inability to adapt to changing human realities. He wrote the state has a role to play in the economy, and specifically, in creating a "safety net." He said: *"There is no reason why in a society which has reached the general level of wealth ours has, the first kind of security should not be guaranteed to all without endangering general freedom, that is: some minimum of food, shelter and clothing, sufficient to preserve health. Nor is there any reason why the state should not help to organize a comprehensive system of social insurance in providing for those common hazards of life against which few can make adequate provision."*

Was the appearance of Reagan's affability and good humor then a hoax? His life story seems to suggest that. In his personal life, he lacked feelings even for his children and was alienated from them. And when his good friend Rock Hudson died from AIDS in 1985, Reagan called AIDS research a "top priority" for his administration; however, he immediately proposed spending levels that cut funds for this research. He spoke warmly but acted coldly. He lacked the will to resist the bidding of the rich who were politically useful to him. The common man was useful only at the voting booth. When that time came, and in public, he unloaded all his charm. He might have failed as an actor but he succeeded in his act of misleading the public.

## 'Supply Side' in the Real World

America's experience in the post-crash years (since 2007-11) shows that corporations would sit on hoards of cash (today they are sitting on a sum of over a trillion dollars), and not create jobs—until they see higher consumer demand. Consumer demand is not increased by laying off public school employees, public school teachers, nurses, or creating jobs outside America, or by dismantling the 'safety net.' Demand is created when consumers have jobs and money to spend. Demand is created by the middle class. But what if the corporations won't spend? Then government expenditure on infrastructure, education, and research is the answer for job creation. It was successfully used by Franklin Roosevelt. It is Economics 101.

## AND WHO GOT THE BLAME FOR REAGAN DEFICITS?

After staggering Reagan deficits, the 1988 Republican Agenda blamed Democrats (who had the majority in Congress) for Reagan's spending: *But the relentless spending of congressional Democrats can undo our best efforts. No president can cause deficits; Congress votes to spend money.*

This Republican version of 'truth' worked—again. HWG Bush won in 1988.

## GHW BUSH

Senior Bush courageously attempted to curb the Reagan deficits so America could regain its position as a leader in the world. He raised taxes and despite demands from his Party to further lower the capital gains, did not do so. He worked to increase federal spending for education, childcare, and advanced technology research, and reauthorized the Clean Air Act, requiring cleaner burning fuels. He signed a law to improve the nation's highway system, and the Immigration Act of 1990 which increased legal immigration by 40 percent. Since he did not lower the taxes for the rich, and did not further "defund" the safety net, he lost favor with the rich and the Religious Right. He lost the 1992 election.

## GW BUSH

### Bush Promise:  From His 2000 Election Agenda:

*We commit ourselves to tax reforms that will sustain our nation's prosperity and reflect its decency. We will reduce the burden on all Americans, especially those who struggle most. We are also determined to protect Medicare and to pay down the national debt. Reducing that debt is...a moral imperative... A Republican president will establish accountability. But make no mistake: In my administration, low-income Americans will have access to high-quality health care.*

### And Bush Record:  Taxes

Bush inherited a surplus from Clinton. He eliminated estate taxes (which affect only the rich after death) and slashed taxes for the rich to the end of 2010 (extended for a year by Obama and set to expire on Dec. 31, 2011 if not made permanent). Between 2001 and 2010 alone, the tax cuts added $2.6 trillion to the public debt. Just servicing the debt created by the tax cuts to the end of 2010 cost the treasury more than $400 billion.

The non-partisan *Congressional Research Service* (CRS) has reported the 10-year revenue loss from extending the 2001 and 2003 tax cuts beyond 2010 at $2.9 trillion, with an additional $606 billion in debt service costs (interest), for a combined total of $3.5 trillion. It is noteworthy that the 75-year Social Security shortfall is about the same size as the cost, over that period, of extending the 2001 and 2003 tax cuts for the richest 2 percent of Americans (those with incomes above $250,000 a year). Members of Congress (mostly from the Tea Party) cannot simultaneously claim that the tax cuts for people at the top are affordable while the Social Security shortfall constitutes a dire fiscal threat.

Just as expected, the Bush tax cuts failed to generate  jobs or to expand the economy. Instead, the tax collections plunged to their lowest share of the economy in last 60 years. While the earnings of people making over $3 million a year, who account for just 0.1 percent of taxpayers, increased by an average of $520,000 a year, the median earnings fell. By 2004, these cuts had reduced federal tax revenues (as a percentage of GDP), to the lowest level since 1959. Eight million jobs were lost during the eight Bush years. On top of it, two wars were started—unfunded--on borrowed money, and tax cuts lavished on the rich--all on borrowed money. If the tax cuts were so good, as the Republicans insist, the economy should have been thriving, instead of going into a tailspin in 2008.

At a time when the country is facing its worst economic downturn in 70 years and more than 25 million are unemployed, it seems inevitable that the "safety net" (Social Security and Medicare programs) would have to be cut because of Bush's war and his "entitlement" program for the rich. The Republicans want the Bush tax cuts to be permanent.  At the end of 2010, Obama was blackmailed into giving an extension of Bush tax cuts by a year in return for an extension of the unemployment benefits.

## Bush Spending

Despite the promise of small government and budget-slashing, Bush expanded public spending by more than 70 percent—more than double the increase under President Clinton. National debt increased by more than $4 trillion—the biggest increase under any president in U.S history. Bush outdid Reagan by far. By the time he left office, the national debt stood at more than $9.849 trillion according to the Treasury figures.

Bush took office in 2001, when the U.S. had a budget surplus. By the time he left, American economy was gasping for breath. *Time* summed it up in January 19, 2009 issue, "George Bush is leaving the White House with a dismal economic record. By almost every measure—GDP growth, jobs, median incomes, financial-market performance—he stacks up as probably the least-successful President on the economic front since Herbert Hoover." In his final White House press conference, he lamented, "Why did the financial collapse have to happen on my watch?" One can sympathize with him—because he had done everything in his power to improve the economy and to balance the budget! What a difference one President can make in downsizing the economy.

Several other things happened under his watch. University of California researchers in '04 found that jobs in the bottom third of the pay scale were growing almost twice as fast as those in the middle. The *New York Times* reported the loss of over 2 million manufacturing jobs between '01 - '04. Gartner Research estimates over 30% of high-tech jobs could be shipped overseas by '15 and University of California researchers estimate up to 14 million jobs are now at risk of outsourcing. But a weak job market is good for breaking the labor unions—one other Republican goal to squash the Democrat's voter base.

Like Reagan, Bush blindly followed the economic and political policies dictated to him by the same Heritage Foundation and the CNP. His cabinet members and other high officials came from

Heritage Foundation and the Federalist Society with one and only one mission: tax cuts for the rich, business deregulation, and increased deficit spending. A *Think Progress* review of the votes in both the House and Senate found that during the Bush term a whopping 130 congressional Republicans voted to hike the debt ceiling by about $4 trillion over 5 years. Not one Republican had the intelligence, guts, or integrity to question it.

While Reagan dumped taxpayers' money on "Star Wars" and on the largest unwarranted military expansion in peace time, Bush misspent on Iraq war on the command of "a higher being." Perhaps, that "higher being" was the CNP. Dick Cheney, his vice president, insisted: "Reagan proved deficits don't matter." *Time* said, "The surest way to get yourself fired as a Bush economic adviser was to say something that was true. Paul O'Neill was ousted from Treasury for warning about deficits."

## The Bush Medicare Benefits: Straight From Machiavelli

Republicans and even the Bush administration supported cuts in Medicare. At a White House talk on Medicare, Bush announced, "We've all come to Washington, those of us who have been elected to office, to serve something greater than our self." To get the senior vote in 2004 elections, Bush cynically expanded Medicare with a drug plan for seniors starting in 2006. He assured public of the bill's $400 billion price tag. When that figure was disputed, his administration admitted it was false.

The bill was rammed through Congress by deceit. The bill was brought to the floor on Saturday evening, November 22, 2003. In the first vote at 3 A.M, the proposal lost by two votes. The Republicans violated House rules, which limit votes to a half hour or less, and proceeded to carry out the longest floor vote in House history—dragging out the tally until 6 A.M, when two Republicans switched their "nays" to "yeas." The bill passed.

Bush's fix was the worst financial blow Medicare has ever suffered. Medicare is now forecast to go bankrupt seven years earlier than previously projected — in 2019, instead of 2026. The trustees forecast that the new prescription drug benefit would cost up to $7 trillion over the next 75 years.

## THE 2008 ECONOMIC MELTDOWN

The causes of the 2007-8 economic meltdown and present unemployment rates and high national debt can be summed up in three lines—one for each Republican president's irresponsible, or brilliant, fiscal policies—depending on your political philosophy.

1. Nixon opened the easy paper money tap by gutting the gold standard,

2. Reagan embraced the conservative think tank's 'supply side' economic theory of low taxes and high spending,

3. GW Bush landed the final blow with the 'free market' doctrine of "large tax cuts for the rich, business deregulation and absence of financial oversight." He topped it with the Iraq war.

During the Bush term, scandals and bankruptcies became common: Enron, WorldCom, Tyco International, Global Crossing, Adelphia Communications. Enron's president—"Kenny boy"—was GW's personal friend. The 2008 collapse of economy was his great "defunding" gift to the Party that had made a President out of a failed life.

## WHAT HAPPENED AFTER 2008?

Obama inherited Afghan and Iraq wars. The costs of the Bush-Obama wars in Iraq and Afghanistan are now estimated to run as high as $4.4 trillion—a major victory for Osama bin Laden, whose declared goal was to bankrupt America. Bush will go down in history as Osama bin Laden's best friend and ally—not the Taliban. The 2011 military budget —almost matching that of the rest of the world combined— is higher in real terms than at any time since World War II and is slated to go even higher.

On top of the two wars, Obama inherited an economy ruined by years of deregulation and lack of financial oversight that cost America $14 trillion in lost wealth and eight million in lost jobs. US Department of Labor estimates that 14 million are unemployed (9.1 %) and millions underemployed. This jobs crisis has sapped federal and state tax receipts and added billions to state budget deficits.

After the 2008 economic meltdown, the GOP spin machine went into hyper-drive to wash the blood from their hands. The party went looking for scapegoats. Tea Party was hurriedly brought into existence to distract the public with talk of national debt. Governors across the nation, backed by Wall Street's Club for Growth and the Koch Brother's Americans for Prosperity, worked hard to convince Americans that the jobs crisis is actually a deficit crisis and that the culprits are not the big banks on Wall Street, but state, county and municipal workers and the labor unions with inflated wages and pensions. In lockstep, state governors began reaching for an almost identical (previously failed) set of "solutions" to the state's financial woes: massive tax breaks for big corporations, constitutional amendments to prevent states from raising revenue, the slashing of critical public services, the busting of unions, and attempts to privatize every possible aspect of government including: prisons, the Post Office, and public schools.

## Is a Poorer Nation Good for GOP?

*A New York Times* (September 29, 2011) article by Jackie Calmes and Mark Landler suggests that lower income and lower educated independent voters tend to favor Republicans. Could this be the reason for Republicans crusade against public education and the middle class? What could be the other reasons?

## GOP: THE 2008 MELTDOWN, "A TERRIFIC OPPORTUNITY"

By December 2008, while the economy was shedding hundreds of thousands of jobs a month, one group of Republicans was treating the national catastrophe as a 'terrific opportunity'. Governor Mitch Daniels, who had served under GW Bush administration, reminded an ALEC gathering of Republican legislators and corporate lobbyists that the collapse of the U.S. economy was *"a terrific time to shrink government!"* Rupert Murdock of Fox News was salivating at the prospect of privatization of public education. He hired Joel Klein in November 2010 as a $2 million-a-year executive vice president from his post as chancellor of New York City's school system to sit on News Corp.'s board of directors and advise the company's entry into the for-profit education market.

 When Obama came to power in 2008, GOP's declared policy was to stop the economy from recovering. Senate minority leader McConnell openly said that his number one goal was to make sure Obama was a one-term president. Sabotaging the economy was good politics: bad economy will lead to Obama's defeat in 2012. Rush Limbaugh said he wanted Obama to fail. It did not matter that millions of Americans—teachers, fireman, working class, children, minorities and the poor —were getting laid off and losing homes across the country during the housing-mortgage crisis. As Reagan had said 'compassionately', the homeless *"make it their own choice for staying out there."* Even if they had been 'pushed out' there?

When he took the oath of Office, Obama's hands were tied by the debt crisis and shrinking revenues.

While showing great concern about national debt reduction, in August, 2011, the House members rejected a deficit-reduction deal that included $1 in tax increases for every $10 in spending cuts. GOP had the opportunity to accept a White House offer to reduce $4 *trillion* deficit. It showed the GOP priorities: deficit reduction was really unimportant. What mattered was that there be no increase in taxes on the rich. It may be loyalty to the no tax "pledge," but it was disloyalty to the nation, and a betrayal of the people.

Grover Norquist, head of Americans for Tax Reform, has bullied elected fellow Republicans for years into signing a pledge that they would never support a tax increase and if they do, they will pay a price. "My God, what has this country come to when one person has to give you permission to do what's best for the country?" Clinton lamented in a recent speech, referring to Norquist.  And who is this Grover Norquist? Living in style, once involved in a corruption scandal with Jack Abramoff and Ralph Reed. He described his agenda for Bush's second term (when Bush was freed from the worry about the next election) as crippling the financial base of the Democratic party by taking down labor unions and tort lawyers. But Norquist is not a free agent—no one in the GOP is—he is only following the orders of his masters. Even Reagan did that. And so did GW Bush.  The GOP callousness and arrogance is based on the assumption that people—including those who think they are smart—can always be hoodwinked by the Republican propaganda machine. The Republican landslide victories in the House in 2010 elections proved that.

Economics correspondent Martin Wolf of the *London Financial Times* wrote on July 13, 2011, "It is not that tackling the US fiscal position is urgent..." He added: "The astonishing feature of the federal fiscal position is that revenues are forecast to be a mere 14.4 percent of GDP in 2011, far below their postwar average of close to 18 percent. Individual income tax is forecast to be a mere 6.3 percent of GDP in 2011. This non-American (referring to himself) cannot understand what the fuss is about: in 1988, at the end of Ronald Reagan's term, (tax) receipts were 18.2 percent of GDP. Tax revenue has to rise substantially if the deficit is to close."

# IX

## TAKE THE CASH AND SHOVE THIS COUNTRY:

## MONEY IN POLITICS

*"I am such an utter failure, father. I could make nothing of my life."*

*"Son, you are not yet fifty. You could still become the President. Go see my Republican friends! They will get you started as governor somewhere."*— Anonymous, Universal Conversations

◎

In every government, money buys influence. But now money controls the U.S government. In addition to the reasons discussed above, other factors have contributed to this.

### ELECTIONS

### The Primaries

An effective campaign requires huge expenditures: campaign staff, consultants, polling, phone banks, mass mailings, travel, meals for volunteers, and advertisements. With the advent of TV, the parties were having trouble raising funds. Until the 1960s, party leaders nominated candidates with little or no input from the public. Following the 1968 election, the Democrats began holding primaries to allow voters to directly nominate the candidates. The Republicans followed suit. Now the candidates are responsible for raising funds for the primaries and, to an extent, even for the elections.

This has opened the way for the rich to field their own candidates. Primaries have also lengthened the election process, and loosened the party discipline. Example: Sen. Nelson (D) of Nebraska has a consistent record of voting against the party.

Even after the primaries, the party's contribution is partial. So candidates now have become fund raising machines.

The late Senator Barry Goldwater from Arizona once said: "Senators and representatives, faced incessantly with the need to raise ever more funds to fuel their campaigns, can scarcely avoid weighing every decision against the questions, 'How will this influence my fundraising?' rather than 'How will this influence national interest?'"

## THE TWO YEAR ELECTION CYCLE WITHOUT TERM LIMITS

The two-year election cycle for House members—along with the absence of term limits—has not only increased the role of money in elections but also given an edge to the incumbent. Elected candidates develop cozy business relationships, and begin to build war chests for the next election. This has led to a marked increase in the re-election rates for congressional incumbents.

Perhaps one unintended effect of the primaries has been to make the candidate sometimes more important to the voter than the party—quite a few independent voters cross the party line to vote for the candidate they like.

## THE ROLE OF SUPREME COURT

### Gutting the Campaign Finance Reform

The *McCain-Feingold* (2002) campaign finance reform Act had raised the legal limits of fund raising but prohibited unregulated contributions to national political parties.  The law was challenged by Republicans. The Party is against all campaign finance reform. In 2006, the Supreme Court held that a Vermont law imposing mandatory limits on spending was unconstitutional. Then, in the landmark case on January 21, 2010—*Citizens United v. Federal Election Commission*—the Supreme Court held that corporations and unions were "persons" and therefore they had the First Amendment rights of "free speech." Free speech right included the right to spend money in election. Now corporations can spend unlimited money in elections.

Republicans hailed the ruling as a tribute to free speech. The ruling turned corporations into persons and money into speech. It also took away the free speech rights of millions who had no money to contribute to elections. In partial dissent, Justice Stevens wrote: *...the distinction between corporate and human speakers is significant. Although they make enormous contributions to our society, corporations are not actually members of it. They cannot vote or run for office. Because they may be managed and controlled by nonresidents...The financial resources, legal structure, and instrumental orientation of corporations raise legitimate concerns about their role in the electoral process.*

President Obama said the ruling undermines the US Republic by giving *"voice to the powerful interests that already drown out the voices of everyday Americans."* The New York Times wrote that the *Citizens United* decision *"strikes at the heart of democracy"* by having *"paved the way for corporations to use their vast treasuries to overwhelm elections and intimidate elected officials into doing their bidding."*

In July 2010, a federal court in *Speechnow.org v. Federal Election Commission* allowed independent expenditure-only committees (super PACS) to raise unlimited amounts of money from individuals, unions, associations and corporations. Supporters or opponents of candidates now can spend unlimited amounts as long as they don't coordinate their activities with the candidates' campaign. Does it make a difference whether the candidate spends money or an "independent" organization does it for him? The law now legitimizes the "behind-the scene" organizations to be set up for a candidate that can misinform, deceive and attack the rival, while the candidate can pretend innocence and helplessness. One such group was behind the Republican *"Swift Boat Veterans for Truth"* ads that knocked out John Kerry in 2004. Such groups proliferated during the 2009 healthcare reform legislation. The White House could not pass into law the government's right to negotiate drug prices, while Wal-Mart does it routinely.

The decision's effect was immediate. The November 2010 election marked the rise of "super PACs," officially known as "independent-expenditure only political action committees." Total spending on the 2010 midterm elections was about $4 billion, including more than $400 million by independent groups. Republicans picked up six seats in the Senate and more than 60 in the House to regain control. Shell-shocked Democrats have now formed their own super PACs in response. Super PACs are going to be big in 2012.

## WALL STREET: THE AMERICAN FRANKENSTEIN?

Time and time again, Wall Street has brought ruin to the nation that has fostered it. The 1929 stock market crash that led to Depression and the housing market meltdown in 2008 are its lasting and ugly monuments. The regulations passed by Roosevelt after 1928 were chipped away by the Republicans under the ideology of "free market" and "supply side" economics beginning with Reagan in 1980. In the last thirty years, Wall Street has grown so powerful that even after the 2008 global recession caused by it, Wall Street has successfully thwarted every attempt by Obama administration to regulate its practices. The government bailed out Wall Street with billions of dollars with no strings attached— because of the Wall Street's political clout. The "too big to fail" financial institutions took the money but did nothing to solve the home mortgage crisis that led to the meltdown. Not one executive has yet been tried for fraud or sent to jail. Wall Street is opposed to all consumer protection laws, shareholder control, tax increases, or curbs on executive remuneration. The "too big to fail" banks are "far bigger" now than before the 2008 crisis. Yet, Wall Street wants to privatize Social Security so it can manage retirement funds and generate billions more in commissions and fees.

The Wall Street personifies the Republican party's "free market" ideology of 'crony capitalism.' Is this the best the Party (according to its faith in the free markets) can do for America?

## THE EFFECT OF MONEY

### Decline in the Quality of Leaders

Suited to the genius of its people, it was the caliber of its leaders that led to America's meteoric rise. Those men loved their country and worked for democracy: democracy that promotes equal economic opportunities for all and unleashes the entrepreneurial spirit of the people. But limiting education, healthcare, and increasing inequality restricts those opportunities to the wealthy. The increasing role of money in politics draws a new breed of politicians dedicated to serving the interests of the rich who dislike democracy. This has affected the quality of leaders.

The large number of evangelicals (followers of the Religious Right ideology created with the help of the rich) vote as a bloc. This has spawned a new breed of conservative politicians who flaunt their religious values by engaging in rhetoric and hypocrisy. They claim to be leaders because of their conservative values. Think Bachman,

131

Cain, Gingrich, Santorum, and Perry. Rev. Pat Robertson ran for presidency in 1988 on the same basis and his 'unimpeachable' morality. He lost to GHW Bush. But it does not matter. For these 'leaders' even losing is profitable--they cash out the increased name recognition by selling books and dvds to their hungry constituency. Newt Gingrich, and Sarah Palin are just two examples.

This use of religion in politics raises several questions. The Constitution provides for separation of Church (religion) and State. Of course, a voter can mix religion and politics as an individual. But what about a candidate seeking public office? What if a Party's political agenda is controlled by its religious ideology? Does it not squarely violate the Constitution? Can a presidential candidate use religion to get elected? Can a President advance a religious ideology through his public policies? It does not appear that these issues have been considered.

The Republican party does not want leaders, it wants stooges who can win the evangelical bloc, and somehow lure enough independent voters who would plant him in the White House. The formula: "conservative values" plus "likability" translates into the criterion of "electability"—which is very similar to "salability" in the used car industry. The car must look and smell good at the time of sale—it matters little how it works later. In the real world, the buyer may succeed in returning the car by taking the seller to court for fraud. Since the voters have no such recourse, fraud in election is risk-free. The President comes with no warranties.

Professing belief in the "free market," "family values" or religion does not turn one into a leader. A leader has to have integrity. More and more, people are demanding integrity even in their food. That's the reason why *Whole Foods* is thriving. A leader looks at the country's problems, its financial situation, at his options, and only then takes action. He does not come pre-programmed with an agenda to benefit the rich.

This gives rise to the question: how do you sell a candidate lacking in leadership qualities? That's where the Republican propaganda machine kicks in. That's where big money moves in. The Party has a devised a method for winning. The Party will savage the opponent with negative ads—these will be more vicious in the brave new 2012 world of super PACs. Campaign managers will skillfully hide the candidate's unsavory record. GW Bush's DUI did not come out almost until the end, and his military record could not be traced at all; the public never learnt about his close ties to the Religious Right and that he was a "Dominionist."

For an interesting take on this, see:
[http://www.yuricareport.com/Dominionism/TheDespoilingOfA merica.htm]

The marvel is that in all national TV debates, not one interviewer had the courage to ask Bush: Are you a Dominionist? This tells a lot about the state of our media. With material information pushed under the rug, Bush got elected on superficial information.

The image-polishers repackage the candidate's weaknesses as 'folksy' qualities that make people feel they can sit down with him and have a chat over a hamburger and fries at McDonalds. That's the image that endeared Reagan to the public. It also sold GW Bush—despite the inerasable smirk and a blustery demeanor untouched by intelligence.

It is no accident that in the last over 30 years, the Republican presidents have come with failed careers--Reagan and GW Bush. GHW Bush may be the only exception. They lacked the self-confidence and the spine that is built by success and achievements before coming to the Office. Of course, the Party has produced

Presidents—but not leaders. These men could not stand up to the Wall Street, or resist the will of their patrons. White House was the reward for their loyalty to the rich. What they did to the country is another story.

The Republican party presidential candidates in the 2012 pre-primaries come injected with the same strain. Even Mitt Romney, a successful businessman, is playing second fiddle to the conservatives. The candidates have not even discussed the nation's problems: healthcare, unemployment, national debt. They attack Obama for all the ills of the country. They boast about their conservative values. As if hanging a few gays and dismantling abortion clinics will create jobs, or solve the national debt crisis. Is this the best America can do? Is this the best the Republican party can do?

## HOW ARE THE ELECTIONS IN BRITAIN CONDUCTED?

The British run their government and their elections like a business. Not for drama or entertainment. Legislation to prevent excessive spending by electoral candidates in the UK has been in place since 1883. The UK system of regulating campaign financing focuses on limiting the expenditure of political parties and individual candidates, and combines a transparent reporting system of donations and expenditures. The election there lasts for about four weeks, and the parties and candidates cannot buy broadcasting time. Every party has to reveal its agenda before the election; the agenda must deal with education, healthcare, economy's growth, and jobs. Many British politicians use facts and figures to highlight problems and make comparisons with the policies or the performance of the opponents. Elections are fought based on a Party's specific agenda. Failure to deliver on promises leads to the party's fall—the Opposition always stands ready to topple the government in power. The Prime Minister can't run or hide even for a month behind his cronies and his lies. But a U.S. president can lie and hide behind his cronies and controlled press conferences for eight years. And then brag about it. GW Bush did it.

# X

## THE FUTURE? BACK TO THE PAST

*The future ain't what it used to be.* —Yogi Berra

Ⓞ

While the Republicans have been busy dismantling the democratic "safety net," the Democrats have been asleep at the wheel. Many have cheerfully voted with the Republicans. There is no Democrat strategic coordinating center to monitor, gather intelligence and frame a quick and effective response. Even after more than thirty years, the Party has been unable to develop an effective argument based on fairness, morality and the American heritage of democratic values. As a result, the Party was shell-shocked in 2000, 2004, and in the mid-term elections in 1994 and 2010.

Let's look at the media. In a democracy, it is media's that keeps the public informed about politics. But the media is interested in sensationalizing world disasters, revolutions, kidnappings and crimes in America. It spends the rest of its time on delivering political information that is readily available. Speculation, meaningless projections, daily polls and endless opinions fill the news. The media's goal is to improve its rating and revenues. Of course, one expects the Fox News to misinform the public. But at least Fox News makes money out of its mission to mislead. That's the mandate it has from the Religious Right. But what about other channels? The result is that the public knows little about the Religious Right ideology, the CNP, the Federalist Society, and the false tax-exemption claims. The CEOs of most corporations subscribe to the Religious Right 'free market' ideology and are members of the CNP; and the corporations are an important source of advertisement revenues. Hence, silence is golden. Let the public figure out the facts.

Uninformed, the people have been voting against their economic-interest for decades. The question for the public is whether the ideology that has drained the wealth of Americans by over $8 trillion and caused the subprime mortgage housing disaster, and led to loss of millions of jobs, is good for America?

## WHERE IS AMERICA HEADED?

Ralph Neas, President of *People for The American Way*, a Christian organization, provided a glimpse of what's in store for Americans when he testified before the House Judiciary Subcommittee on the Constitution, October 10, 2002:

*"Mr. Chairman,*

*The two-prong strategy of the right-wing of the Republican Party is simple but breathtakingly radical. First, enact a permanent tax cut which will eliminate $6 trillion in revenue over the next 20 years. That will in effect starve the federal government so it will be unable to fund many vital governmental functions performed since the New Deal.*

*The second prong is to pack the federal judiciary with right-wing ideologues whose judicial philosophy would turn back the clock on civil rights, environmental protections, religious liberty, reproductive rights and privacy and so much more. Take away the money. And then take away legal rights that have been part of our constitutional framework for 65 years. We do indeed need a national debate. Before the American people wake up one morning and discover that their fundamental rights and liberties have vanished overnight."*

If it sounded futuristic in 2002, in 2012 America is closer to it.

Bill Moyers, an acclaimed TV journalist, in his address at Union Theological Seminary in New York on September 10, 2005, commented on what Americans need to do is to come to grips with the dangerous, anti-democratic Christian Right. He said, *"Democrats are divided and paralyzed, afraid that if they take on the organized radical right they will lose what little power they have...As I look back on the conflicts and clamor of our boisterous past, one lesson about democracy stands above all others: Bullies— political bullies, economic bullies and religious bullies—cannot be appeased; they have to be opposed with a stubbornness to match their own. This is never easy; these guys don't fight fair... But freedom on any front—and especially freedom of conscience—never comes to those who rock and wait, hoping someone else will do the heavy lifting."* He added, *"The country is not yet a theocracy but the Republican Party is, and they are driving American politics, using God as a battering ram on almost every issue: crime and punishment, foreign policy, health care, taxation, energy, regulation, social services and so on."*

The problem is not with the Religious Right but with the 'free market' capitalist ideology stuffed inside the Religious Right ideology that has wrecked the economy. After 30 years of relentless assault on their economic wellbeing, annually increasing education costs and soaring health insurance premiums, are Americans close to realizing the bitter truth? The 99% movement shows the first sign of public awareness. Will the movement succeed in the teeth of the Republican propaganda? Don't hold your breath.

## HOW TO VOTE IN 2012?

The thesis of the Republican party is that people with low income are indifferent to politics and do not vote; they can be crucified without consequences. For such voters it is important to show up at the voting booth and vote. Only they can save themselves by asserting their voice. No one is looking out for them. It is important to vote; each vote carries the same weight as that of Bill Gates.

For others, it is not hard to decide for whom to vote in 2012. Just ask three questions: 1. Who has the Republican party economically benefitted in the last three decades? 2. What has it done for jobs, education and healthcare? 3. Are the Republican policies creating better opportunities for the next generation?

There is great buzz about 'personal responsibility' on the rightwing propaganda machine. What about the capitalists' personal and social responsibility? Has not the American society— its educated and hardworking work force, its purchasing power, its educational institutions, its protection of intellectual property, its infrastructure—contributed to their wealth? What is their personal responsibility to this society? Warren Buffet should know, and he says the rich should pay higher taxes in the interest of fairness.

The 2012 election is critical. America stands at a crossroads. One more Republican victory in the White House could put America back by 100 years. It sounds ridiculous. But think where America would be today had GW Bush not been the President during 2000-2008? He set back America by eight trillion dollars—the debt that the future generations will have to pay.

## THE SOLUTION

It matters little what a writer puts down on paper. The important thing is public awareness. So some ideas are worth kicking around. There are three solutions—the immediate and the practical, medium term and perhaps doable, and the long term that may take another fifty years.

### The Immediate Solution

The best solution for people is to go out and vote. Take down the Republican members of the House and the Senate who have signed the Tax Pledge, and violated their oath to the Constitution. Once the House and Senate members realize that they were not elected to serve the rich, they would do what is right. For a list of the House members and senators who have signed the pledge, see: http://s3.amazonaws.com/atrfiles/files/files/120111-federalpledgesigners.pdf.

For a list of state representatives and governors, see: http://www.atr.org/taxpayer-protection-pledge

### The Medium-Term Solution

It requires no protracted Constitutional Amendment. The parties started the primary system in 1968 and the parties can eliminate it. Is it too late? And the parties can eliminate the filibuster rule on their own, and tighten party discipline.

The national TV stations should be required by FCC in their licensing agreements to set aside 5-7% free broadcast time for public issue debates. This should be combined with campaign finance reform.

There are two kinds of election systems. Currently, the US has single-member districts, and winner-take-all style of elections, in which the votes cast for the loser go down the drain. As a result, the minority voters have no representation in the legislature. This leads to voter apathy, especially among the minorities who feel marginalized. Among the 21 democracies in Western Europe and North America, the US is next to last in the voter turn-out.

This system was devised by the major political parties in the U.S to keep the minorities out from the legislature. Winner-take-all elections are also more susceptible to the corruption of big money.

The other system, used by most of the world's democracies, is proportional representation (PR). Under this system, all political groups win seats in legislature in proportion to their strength in the electorate. PR style is based on the principle of fair representation.

It may be time to think about a third party. Third parties face overwhelming odds in the US. In all states, while the Democratic and Republican candidates automatically get on the ballot, third-party candidates have to get thousands of signatures just to be listed on the ballot. Also, third-party candidates often face financial difficulties because a party must have received at least 5 percent of the vote in the previous election to qualify for federal funds. The existing two parties have a strong incentive to protect the duopoly. The current two-party system is partly responsible for the poor shape of American democracy.

## The Long Term Solution: A Comprehensive Constitutional Reform

Any sensible amendment would be fiercely opposed by the Republicans, especially the Senate, whose first loyalty is now to the rich.

- Eliminate the Senate. At the minimum, neuter it. Make it an advisory body.

- Include a section on political parties, require parties to formulate and disclose a specific agenda limited to economy, jobs, healthcare, public education, defense, infrastructure, and the environment. Elections should be funded by federal and state governments.
- Eliminate the two yearly elections, and replace them with elections every four years—concurrent with the presidential election.
- Limit the senators and House members to two four year terms.
- The Supreme Court should be divested of its power to rule on the constitutionality of Congressional Acts.
- The president should be elected by popular vote. Remove the Electoral College.
- A provision to remove the president by majority of votes—60 or 66 percent—of the House should be there for not delivering on his party's agenda, or pursuing an agenda not disclosed during the campaign. Eliminate the impeachment provision which has no teeth.

## SOME USEFUL WEBSITES

The websites are a great resource—if one has no time limit. Only a few are listed below.

[http://www.yuricareport.com/Dominionism/TheDespoilingOf America.htm.]

Katherine Yurica's website provides an incisive analysis on Dominionism, GW Bush, Machiavelli etc.

http://www.talk2action.org/

www.theocracywatch.org

http://americantheocracy.org/

Americans United for Separation of Church and State

http://alecexposed.org/wiki/ALEC_Exposed

http://www.takeoverworld.info/cnplinks.html

https://www.rutherford.org/

http://watch.pair.com/moon.html

http://www.seekgod.ca/cnp.htm

http://www.conspiracyarchive.com/Commentary/CNP_Domini onism.htm

http://www.rawstory.com/news/2006/Exclusive_Reagan_cons ervative_lashes_out_at_0728.html

http://www.rightweb.irc-online.org/articles/display/World_Anti-Communist_League#P10604_2126989

Right Wing Watch

Dispatches from the Culture Wars

Spiritual Politics

Outing Dominionism

Dark Christianity

http://www.publiceye.org/apocalyptic/Dances_with_Devils_1.html

http://www.alternet.org/news/145796/

http://www.salon.com/news/feature/2009/07/21/c_street/

http://www.time.com/time/covers/1101050207/photoessay/4.html

http://en.wikipedia.org/wiki/Christian_Reconstructionism

http://www.motherjones.com/politics/2005/12/nation-under-god

http://www.religiousrightwatch.com/2006/10/christian_recon.html

http://www.npr.org/templates/story/story.php?storyId=102005062&ps=bb1

http://www.motherjones.com/media/2009/03/books-purpose-driven-wife

http://www.jewsonfirst.org/patriarchy.php

http://www.publiceye.org/portal/top-domtheo-page.html

http://barthsnotes.wordpress.com/

http://nyarbb.com/kyep/links-kye.html#major

http://www.conjure.com/right.html

# BIBLIOGRAPHY

## Constitution

Miracle At Philadelphia: The Story of the Constitutional Convention May-September 1787 (1986) by Catherine Drinker Bowen. For a good background of the delegates' personalities in the drama.

Novus Ordo Seclorum-The Intellectual Origins of the Constitution (1985) by Forrest McDonald. A good resource for the origins of the Constitution.

How Democratic is the American Constitution (2001) by Robert Dahl-Sterling Professor emeritus of political science at Yale.

The Senate: The Most Exclusive Club: A History of the Modern United States Senate (2006) by Lewis Gould

Original Intent & the Framers of the Constitution (1994) by Harry Jaffa

Storm over the Constitution (1999) by Harry Jaffa

## Politics, Parties, and the Economy

There is no all-encompassing book. There are dozens of books on the subject, each has an angle. A few are listed below.

Winner-Take-All Politics: How Washington Made the Rich Richer—and Turned Its Back on the Middle Class (2011) by Jacob S. Hacker, Paul Pierson

The Triumph of Politics: Why the Reagan Revolution Failed (1986) by David Stockman

Machiavelli on Modern Leadership: Why Machiavelli's Iron Rules Are As Timely And Important Today As Five Centuries Ago (2000) by Michael Ledeen

It Takes a Pillage: An Epic Tale of Power, Deceit, and Untold Trillions (2010), by Nomi Prins

Aftershock: The Next Economy and America's Future (2011), by Robert Reich.

Reich was Labor Secretary under Bill Clinton and is currently a professor at UC, Berkeley. His knowledge about the economy is encyclopedic. Reich draws the parallels between the Great Depression and the economic meltdown, the imbalance of wealth, the squeezing of the middle class.

The Emerging Republican Majority (1969) by Kevin Phillips

For more than thirty years, Kevin Phillips' has recorded the history of American politics and economics. He is a former Nixon staffer and Republican strategist, and current radio/TV commentator who left the Republican fold for academia. Other books by Kevin Phillips include:

The Politics of Rich and Poor: Wealth and the American Electorate in the Reagan Aftermath (1991),

Boiling Point: Democrats, Republicans, and the Decline of Middle-Class Prosperity (1994),

Wealth and Democracy: A Political History of the American Rich (2003),

American Theocracy: The Peril and Politics of Radical Religion, Oil, and Borrowed Money in the 21st Century (2007),

Bad Money: Reckless Finance, Failed Politics, and the Global Crisis of American Capitalism (2008)

# INDEX

## About the Author

A U.C. Berkeley law grad, the author is a retired businessman. He practiced law for many years, and has also previously published a novel. He spent a year at Harvard Law School at its invitation, and was published in the Harvard Int'l Law Journal. He lives in the Silicon Valley area with his wife.


\*\*\*                                 \*\*\*                                 \*\*\*


Dear Reader: This book is a labor of love. If you liked it, please tell your friends. And please leave your comments on Amazon. You will be helping others. It will be appreciated.

Your suggestions are welcome. Pl. forward to:

kushnersam@yahoo.com

Thanks.

www.ingramcontent.com/pod-product-compliance
Lightning Source LLC
Chambersburg PA
CBHW071329310526
45789CB00017B/2015